T0368386

YOU CAN'T BLAME KARMA

The Ultimate Guide
To Breaking Free From The Patterns
That Hold You Back

SKY STEVENS

Balboa Press books may be ordered through booksellers or by contacting:

Balboa Press
A Division of Hay House
1663 Liberty Drive
Bloomington, IN 47403
www.balboapress.com
844-682-1282

Cover design created on Canva by Sky Stevens
Armor Image by Gordon Johnson from Pixabay
Gear image by TheDigitalArtist from Pixabay

Print information available on the last page.

ISBN: 979-8-7652-5746-3 (sc)
ISBN: 979-8-7652-5747-0 (e)

Balboa Press rev. date: 03/29/2025

DEDICATION

I dedicate this book to those on a journey back to their authentic nature. Those magnificent warriors who dare to pursue a different life. Those with the courage to unveil every aspect of their being and live in it, boldly. Those who dare to want more, to have more and to be more. I salute you all.

The Authentic Life Alliance is a group
of individuals worldwide
who dedicate themselves to living in
the highest version of SELF.
This is the greatest gift we can offer the world.

At the Authentic Life Alliance, we believe that each
of us has a gift to bring to the world and we all have
lessons to learn. We take responsibility for what we have
created in our lives and support each other to rise up to a
new level of being. We coach, teach and learn from each
other's progress. Join us.

authenticlifealliance@outlook.com

Close to Self

I speak my truth in all I say,
I honor myself in every way.
My heart is open. My eyes are wide.
All I am now comes alive!

Authentic Self, I rise to meet.
Head held high. The trust complete.
Open to receive and give.
Today is when I really live!

Close to heart, I find the key,
Unlocking all my mystery.
All life's gifts now come my way,
All I am, is here to stay.

No more doubt, all fear dissolved.
All the past is now resolved.
Open now to gratitude,
Yes....this is now the life I choose.

-Sky Stevens

TABLE OF CONTENTS

Preface...xiii
Introduction..xxiii
Before You Get Started xxvii
Suggestions To My Readers.........................xxix

Part I The Inner Workings of Belief Formation

Chapter 1   Four Layers of Beliefs............................. 1
Chapter 2   Beliefs and the Synthetic Self................. 13

Part II What Beliefs Create

Chapter 3   Behind the Scenes of the Synthetic Self...35
Chapter 4   Life in the Synthetic Self..........................51

Part III The Road Map for Change

Chapter 5   Redefining Self Through the Scope
             of Concern Pyramid 69

Part IV Creating a Life Beyond Belief

Chapter 6   Learning to Live in the Natural Self........ 93
Chapter 7   Growing into More. the Shift from
             Image to Identity....................................109
Chapter 8   Altering Intent 123
Chapter 9   Learning to Trust the Natural Self 145
Chapter 10   12 Simple Ways to Stay True to
             Yourself Every Day 165

About the Author...193

PREFACE

People say things happen for a reason, but as I walked along the beach that fall morning, the reason was lost behind a wall of ego. I was deep in thought, pondering my conditioning and the ideals of the human herd that had raised me.

Typically, I moved with the herd unaffectedly. But today I felt detached and adrift like a helium balloon untethered. The day before, I had been downsized (that's what my boss called it) from a job deep in the heart of the status quo. A job I didn't like. A job I had no desire or interest in doing. A job that defined me within the human herd. A job I had been doing for over 5 years. I was walking to clear the angst from my ego, the self-pity from my psyche. I walked to consider how I had lasted so long at that job. Why I had first agreed to do it. How I was going to explain my sudden unemployment to the herd. And what I was going to do with the rest of my life.

As I walked along the beach, I realized I had learned to be grateful for the crumbs of inclusion that were dropped before me. I gobbled them up like a feast. My caregivers drilled it into me to be grateful for the leftover attention, the hand-me-down interest, the scraps of care I was offered. And I believed it was the best I would ever get or deserve or warrant. Yes, I believed them. The job was a crumb I had scrambled towards. It was the "I will accept being benched because at least I'm on the team" life I had created for myself to keep that conditioning in place. It was the Covert belief, nestled at the core of my self-image, and I had built a life I didn't want around it. My feet stopped as the revelation consumed my focus. I had believed it and had justified that belief. I had positioned myself as a benched player, waiting for the coach to recognize my worth. The corner office was the bench, and the coach was my employer. The other players were my family, and I was trying to gain validation from them to emboss me with worthiness. What if, instead of scrambling for crumbs, or sitting on the bench, I made my own feast and played my own game? What if I stopped playing 'less than' and stepped into the spotlight of my life?

I left the beach and headed along the sidewalk while cars raced passed me. I suspected it was around seven a.m. and folks were making their way to their status quo jobs. Jobs they didn't like. Jobs they had no desire or interest in doing. Jobs that limited them to the conditioning they had received and the beliefs they held about themselves. I wondered how many of those people felt fulfilled or excited about what they were doing with their lives.

A wave of shame washed over me as my conditioning took center stage. Suddenly, every one of those people in those cars heading to the job they didn't like could see me through my herd's eyes with a neon sign over my head that read 'unemployed failure'. The shame felt so strong I could already picture myself in bed with a tub of Haagen-Dazs.

Determined to get a grip on my festering emotions, I

moved in the opposite direction. My head raging the battle between ingrained conditioning and another way of being.

I did a quick check in. I didn't feel any different today than I did yesterday. Physically, I felt the same. Mentally and emotionally, I was ok. There was a new spring in my step at the realization I had more than enough money to keep a roof over my head and food on the table for the next few years, yet still, the shame of not working was so heavy that I could feel my shoulders drop under its weight. So, if self-sufficiency wasn't the issue, where was all this shame coming from? Was it from the interruption in the flow of money coming in? Was it about the capability of earning? Was it the sudden lack of title and reputation? What was that voice that said I had just lost everything? That voice, it turned out, was not mine. It was far more familiar than my voice. It was my father's.

People work. That's what people do. They work to live. And if one doesn't do what others do, if one doesn't work, they are not a person. That was my father's thinking. Raised on the wrong side of the tracks, he had a strong work ethic and a dependence on an employer to dictate when his workday ended, and his life could begin. He was the youngest of his herd and had learned his place on the lowest rung of the value ladder. Work had given him the worthiness he lacked at home. "You must work to live", he always said. Now I realize he was saying "You must work to be seen".

My mother defined a person by the position or title they held. Now that work didn't exist for me, there was no nameplate on my desk, no status, and no me. My mother, also conditioned to be less than like my father, lived with the stigma of being a perpetual disappointment. From the right side of the tracks, though the wrong side of gender significance, she refined my father's message by hand-picking suitable careers that would generate acceptable income while contributing to the raising of personal and family image. The bottom line of my herd was that one did not exist as a person until they gained validation through not just work, but through an established and prestigious career.

With all that conditioning crammed into my learned self-image, did the end of this job mean I had ceased to exist? How long would it take my herd to re-calculate my worth in the absence of this job? Would they still see me, or would I become as invisible as I had been before I hoisted myself up the rungs of worthiness on the corporate ladder? An emptiness washed over me as I came to terms with the only logical conclusion. In their eyes, I was no longer fit to be seen. I still had an IQ of 132 and two university degrees. I still was creative, intelligent and outgoing. I was still the same person. Still vibrant, passionate, and caring. Regardless, though, the minute this job ended, I instantly became less than.

I suddenly realized I was standing still. Somewhere in my inner conflict, I had stopped walking as if I had consumed all the energy it took to propel myself forward. Why was I still functioning when everything I had learned about me suggested I shouldn't be? What was the purpose of my existence? Surely there must be more to it than getting up, going to work, coming home, going to bed. Surely there must be more to me than a distorted image validated through employment. Yet if I dared to remove the beliefs of the herd from my mind, what remained? Certainly, this was not the first time I had been unemployed, nor I suspect, would it be the last. Reassuring myself that I had survived this experience before, and the sky had not fallen, I continued my walk.

When I really thought about it, I realized it was not surprising that I would harbor beliefs about work, given the influences of my conditioning. What I also realized was that, at my core, I had no desire to adhere to the level of status and inclusion of such conditioning. Had I subconsciously sabotaged myself from establishing a prestigious career as a way of remaining unsuitable to enter the ring, never mind fight with the lions? As long as I didn't show my potential to land a status-defining career, I was off the hook. I was saved from the pressure of working my way up to inclusion and upholding the family name. After all, I had watched my older siblings climb the rungs of the corporate ladder and it seemed to me that none of those rungs won them a pat on the back. When they jumped through one hoop, there was always another waiting for them. Were they happy? Did they value personal expression, fulfillment, or self-mastery? They were always striving, always wanting, always achieving, always climbing. As the youngest of the herd, it had been safest to just take myself out of that equation.

I could do it I suppose. I could return my focus to striving for the corner office with a view. I could force myself to want what my human herd offered and held sacred. Then I would never have to feel this way again. I would never have the fear of abandonment and exclusion. I would never have to face my unworthiness, my non-existence. I would be celebrated, included, and safe. With great resolve, I mentally plotted my next steps to regain my footing on the worthiness ladder. After all, if I had a new position, the fallout from the loss of the old one would be minimized.

Returning to my physical body, I realized I was in the woods. Somehow, I had covered over a mile of distance and shifted from the road to the forest without even noticing. A small grove of Alder trees stood about four feet in front of me and half-consciously, I covered the remaining distance to its center. The other half of my consciousness was fervently piecing together the steps I needed to secure that corner office.

Then, something remarkable happened. A voice seemed to rise from the trees and surround me. "Is it who you are?" the voice asked. My hackles went up. "Of course, it is who I am. Of course, the herd defines me. Who else would? I am part of the herd. I was born into it. I have been fighting it because I was afraid to succeed." But as the message sank in, my defenses were silenced. My knees buckled, and I felt the ground softly catch me. I wept. A whisper threaded its way through the sobs. "It isn't who I am. I just believed it. All of it. I believed everything I learned about me. I believed in the identity that was created for me. I believed I was unworthy as a person, and it was necessary to be prestigiously employed to be seen."

Suddenly it all became clear. All the lies I had told myself. All the bogus ideals I had held myself accountable to. The fear of not being good enough was not about being good enough at all. It wasn't even about me. It was about being an accessory to the herd; a bright bobble that would elevate the herd's status. In essence, I had twisted my square pegged self into the herd's round hole to elevate the herd's status. It hadn't ever been about me as a person. In fact, nothing I believed about myself was personal. Not one belief was actually about who I authentically was. I had simply believed every message passed down to me, just as my parents believed every message passed down to them and their parents believed what was passed to them.

I swear I lost fifty pounds that day; twenty pounds from the weight of keeping myself down, ten pounds of comparisons and fighting to be good enough, five pounds of guilt and fifteen pounds of the negative thoughts I couldn't even define. On that day, as my physical body lay crumbled in a heap on the mossy forest floor, a less defined version of me rose and danced in the trees.

I considered the useful adaptions I had applied to my true self to survive the environment of my conditioning. The fact is, I had been applying them for years, working jobs I didn't like, achieving titles I didn't want, all to be noticed and included by the environment of my birth.

Could there be more to life than simply appeasing the herd?

By the time I returned home, I was determined to find out. If I could separate every thought, word and action of mine from every thought, word and action I learned from my human herd, I would know for sure. In short, I was on a mission to separate who I truly was from who I had learned to be. And, I resolved with a heavy sigh, to let the chips fall where they may.

As I considered the difference between my true SELF and my learned identity, I stumbled upon a text that suggested health is a combination of what you eat and what's eating you. This gave me rise to ponder. Though I had improved much of my diet and exercise over the years because appearance was important to the herd, I had, admittedly, spent little time examining what I allowed to eat at me. The herd did not discuss such things. But, I realized, that day in the Alder grove, I allowed a great deal to eat away at me. I allowed so much to eat away at me in fact, I hadn't even noticed I had entered the forest. The truth was, my conditioning, all those old patterns that had been passed down, all those beliefs I had stored, had been eating away at me for most of my life. All the trying and striving to run with the herd nearly consumed my authentic self whole. It was barely distinguishable. Only when I consciously determined to extract who I was from who I had learned to be could I see the vast difference.

What if such a Self Un-Covery process, a willingness to define who I truly am independent of the herd, allowed me to exist beyond the environment of my birth? What would my life be like void of the herd's conditioning? What if I had the courage to reveal all that I am? What if I give my SELF permission to steer my experiences instead of the herd steering my life? What if I could do more than hover over this emotional poverty line? What if I could truly live?

People say things happen for a reason. What if things happen to teach us to distinguish ourselves from the herd, to locate our truth, our SELF, and follow our purpose? What if the reason things happen is to teach us to own our own journey?

INTRODUCTION

You can feel it, can't you, as you go about your daily life, the nagging feeling that you were meant for more? You knew it as a child, and you dreamed big. What happened to those big dreams? Are they your reality today or did they get pushed aside for society approved matters like earning a living, getting an education, fashioning a career, joining the family business or having a family of your own? Still, though, in the night's silence, you dive into the realm of endless possibilities and wonder what could have been.

My dreams were not my reality either. Raised by corporate parents, the striving for career, image, and status, is what defined me as a person and I built my life around that. I stumbled my way up the corporate ladder to the corner office with a view. The herd was proud, but I spent more time gazing out the window, wondering what else was out there, than doing my job.

Was this it? Was this all there was to my life? Something deep inside me said NO. The life I was living had backed me into a corner and only one of us would survive. Leaving was impossible. The only thing more impossible than leaving was staying. Yet was I willing to give up everything I was today for all that I could be? Could I really do it? Just walk out and leave it all behind. No safety net, just leap. I wasn't ready for change. But as I stared out the window of that corner office, I found myself fast-forwarding to the end of my life. Was I lying on my deathbed knowing, with certainty, I had been true to myself? Was I taking my last breath, content that I had fulfilled my life's purpose? Had I explored every aspect of my being, every grain of my potential, every experience, every adventure? Had I lived every day to its fullest? Or was I laying there filled with remorse? Never knowing myself, never facing the fear. Regretting the chances I didn't take, the opportunities I had let slip by. What if there was a whole different life out there for me and I had let fear keep me from living it? What if I could have more, do more, be more?

It was no longer a choice. I had to know before my deathbed came. I was like a snake needing to purge its skin. A skin that no longer fits. A skin that was never mine. A skin that had never truly defined me. It was time to reveal the 'me' that lay underneath. I had to view myself through my own eyes, instead of everyone else's.

Right now, you are catching glimpses of the 'you', you always knew was in there, and this book inspires the persistence to expand those glimpses into reality. This is the perfect time to read *You Can't Blame Karma*. You are exactly where you need to be, in exactly the right moment, with exactly the right tool.

It is time to be curious. Curious to know all you can be, all you can accomplish and who you really are. *You Can't Blame Karma* takes you back to the beginning. It identifies and explores the layers of beliefs, how they were formed, and why. It presents you with the opportunity to shed the skin you learned to wear. You don't have to go on a life-altering road trip to alter your life. You can do it right where you are.

You Can't Blame Karma gives you the tools to harness the thoughts that shape your current reality and release the beliefs behind those thoughts. There are interactive exercises at the back of every chapter to support this, with a final chapter outlining twelve simple ways to stay true to yourself every day. It is the complete process, from start to finish. Where beliefs come from, how to select and release them, how to uncover your truth and how to live in that truth every day.

BEFORE YOU GET STARTED

Before you get started on this book, and thus, find the strength and power to trust your SELF completely, I ask you to consider the following:

1. That all you believe about yourself might be a lie.
2. That your truth is the part of you that does not require a physical form. That innate wisdom, knowledge and intelligence must be your shepherd.
3. That you must be willing to give up everything you are, for everything you may become.

As a child, you believed everything you were told, taught and learned about yourself. What you did or didn't deserve, could or could not have and what you would or wouldn't be. You shaved off the pieces of you that were not suitable for inclusion or care and built an identity from what remained. You have viewed yourself, your life and all your experiences through that lens ever since. Now, through this book, you can break that old lens, reclaim your truth and be who you were born to be.

SUGGESTIONS TO MY READERS

I won't sugar-coat the process laid out within this book. It will make you dig deep. It will locate the pieces of you that were left behind along the way. It will invite you to reclaim your true, authentic nature. It will move you from complacency to truly living. Where it refers to self, it refers to you as you are now. Where it refers to SELF, it refers to the greatest potential of the highest version of you. In essence, all that you can possibly be and all that you have the capacity to be. SELF is a version of you that is beyond your wildest dreams, yet well within the possibilities of your current life. You must give yourself permission to shift from self to SELF. That is all it takes to make your ordinary life extraordinary.

I have set up this book in the order that I learned it. As an evolution of sorts. I have presented each step in the same order that I discovered and applied them to my life. By the time you have finished this book, you will have changed the way you see yourself and how you show up in the world. You are strong and powerful. The chapters ahead will prove it to you. The lessons I learned that stripped off my learned self-image, my Synthetic Self, I pass along to you as exercises located at the back of each chapter. These exercises will cause the 'you' of the past to fall away to reveal the glorious, radiant being you innately are.

I suggest you read this book all the way through. Then

read it again, slowly, doing each exercise with the utmost honesty.

I suggest getting yourself a journal before you start. Not only will the practice of writing actively engage the body and help release any old emotions that linger within, but it will show you what inspires you, as well as your process as you go through the book. Express yourself in any way you wish in your journal. With colored markers, sketches, quotes that inspire you, photos, drawings… anything you want. You can even decorate the cover as a dedication to your journey. So go ahead, be creative, embrace whatever shows up for you and write it down.

I suggest patience. Be generous with yourself. The road back to you is long and uncomfortable. You will have to face some very real truths about yourself that you may not wish to see. The quicker you accept these, the faster you can move on to the life you've always wanted. Holding on to the tried and true just because it is comfortable is how you got here. It serves no other purpose than to keep you stuck. When facing such truths be tolerant and compassionate with your process. Your Natural Self has been with you all along. This book will reveal it to you. It is a process to separate the 'you' you've never met from the 'you' you've learned to be. So be patient and kind to yourself. The results will amaze you!

PART I

THE INNER WORKINGS OF
BELIEF FORMATION

1

FOUR LAYERS OF BELIEFS

"Your life is absolute abundance and the
only thing preventing you from seeing it
is the lens you are looking through."
-Sky Stevens

Yesterday's beliefs sculpt today's decisions. They are the architects of your present, crafting your perceptions and decisions and guiding your current reality. Distinguishing between thoughts, emotions and the different beliefs that steer you is the key to mastering a profound connection with your true SELF. Your past beliefs are not just memories; they are the guiding compass of your present. By unraveling the intricate relationship between thoughts, emotions, and beliefs, you can forge a deeper connection with your authentic SELF and discard the limitations and restrictions that keep your present life immobile.

The connection between your beliefs, thoughts, and emotions is not complex. Beliefs form the thoughts that trigger emotion. The beliefs at the heart of your thoughts and emotions ultimately create your reality and make the difference between a life of utter joy and one of constant confusion and angst. For your beliefs are formed by the level of acceptance you, as a child, consented to apply to everything you were told, taught, or learned consciously or subconsciously. Your thoughts are dependent on the context of those beliefs and can change when your beliefs do. To re-write your story and ultimately create the life you want, you must learn to distinguish between your Collective, Midpoint and Exclusive beliefs and know the relationship between them.

Collective beliefs navigate you through the society in which you were raised. These are society-approved ways of thinking that are accepted by the collective and instilled by your caregivers on behalf of society. The norms, values, and acceptable behaviors of society are all Collective beliefs. They offer the illusion of inclusion through conformity within society.

One example of a Collective belief is that blood is better. Those related by blood are nicer, better, smarter, and more deserving of one's time and energy than those who are not. Blood relations are more important than others and are thus offered the inclusion, acceptance and protection of the pack. Judgments are cast differently for blood relations than for outsiders. Should an outsider treat you poorly, you are free to discount them and end the association. However, if the same treatment comes from a blood relation, it is to be tolerated, justified, excused and even forgiven.

The blood is better belief is a prejudice consciously taught to the young of society. Genetics determine treatment. The shape of the eyes, the contour of the fingers or the texture of the hair are the short cut for an inclusive treatment plan. Those fully engaged in the belief are identified by the label *family*. This defines individual groups who openly consent to the blood is better belief and accept blood relations as the gatekeepers of their lives. In essence, a built-in safety net. Those labeled *family* according to this belief, will always be there to support you, coddle you, rescue you, agree with you, instruct you, look out for you, guide you and most importantly, define you.

Meet Gavi. Gavi was three years old, squatting on the walkway slabs that led to the front door of the child's home. Between the slabs, a colony of ants were hustling and bustling about as the child watched in amazement. When the child's chubby finger covered the ant hole with dirt, the ants began digging their way through to the surface by reconstructing the hole. Gavi asked the ants why they bothered and listened intently to how each had a specific role to fulfill as they worked together for the greater good of the community.

Father smiled as he watched his child explore the ant hill from the door. But when he overheard the conversation, he rushed to the child's side. He gripped the youngster's ear and demanded to know what was going on. Without hesitation Gavi excitedly detailed the conversation with the ants. The father quickly looked up and down the street before marshalling his child into the house and closing the door. Sternly he said, "Don't EVER tell anyone you talk to ants or you'll be locked away in the loony bin!".

To Gavi, talking to the ants was no different than talking to butterflies, plants, dogs or humans. The child talked and listened to every form of life as if it was the most natural thing in the world. It was as natural as the bond between child and father. Until now.

Through the process of learning Collective beliefs in your early years, you inadvertently stumbled over the Midpoint beliefs considered common practice within your specific early environment. Midpoint beliefs are created through pain points, (Father's reaction to Gavi and the ants), often using consequences (the loony bin) to teach basic environmental standards. Such standards apply to all members of the household such as 'removing your shoes when you come in the house' or 'don't talk with your mouth full'. The Midpoint beliefs you learned stemmed from your caregiver's interpretation of Collective beliefs and were responsible for the thought practices and coping mechanisms that determined inclusion and care towards you, as a child.

Not only had Gavi's father allowed Collective beliefs to steer his reaction, but he injected Midpoint beliefs into the equation resulting in a judgement. He then turned that judgment toward his child outlining a punishment for a crime he perceived against his ingrained standards. Unaware of the internal struggle within the father's beliefs, to the child, no crime had taken place. All was as it should be. Except that Gavi had learned the Collective belief that parents looked out for and loved their children no matter what, and since father's reaction to his child was so ferocious, it must mean he was seeing something in Gavi that was so wretched it deserved to be locked up. Gavi's sense of safety was immediately replaced with a haunting uncertainty. Instantly, Gavi had to choose between a father's embrace and an instinct to survive. Determined to stay out of the loony bin, or have father find anything else that might put his child there, Gavi avoided father while silently swearing to conceal everything that came naturally and become someone worthy of remaining in the home.

The Midpoint beliefs of your caregiver are passed along in the form of opinions, judgments and fears. And despite your generation's declaration that you are nothing like your parents, when it comes to Midpoint beliefs, you are, in fact, very much like those who raised you. You emulated the Midpoint beliefs of your caregiver through trial and error, correction and discipline, observation and mirroring, for inclusion's sake, with a special focus on the individual who was most influential for you as a child. How that person defined and demonstrated success is how you define and demonstrate success. How that person identifies and exhibits joy is how you identify and exhibit joy. Disappointment and failure are likewise mimicked. Such conditioning becomes so ingrained it is assumed to be a natural part of your character. But nothing could be further from the truth. For, the Midpoint beliefs witnessed in your early years are the same Midpoint beliefs that were

Sky Stevens

witnessed in the early years of each of your caregivers, and each of their caregivers before that, and so on back in time. Gavi's father, in his childhood, had brushed against the consequences of his caregiver's Midpoint beliefs and had spent his life committed to living under the radar. He had brushed his own child up against the consequences of his Midpoint beliefs and his child committed to living under the radar from that day on.

Once submerged in the Midpoint beliefs of your caregivers, all other possibilities fade from reasoning and your innate self is forfeited in some way for inclusion's sake. By adopting your caregiver's Midpoint beliefs as your own, you also adopt the expression of those Midpoint beliefs. Typically portrayed through behaviors, patterns, judgments and opinions as personal interpretations of Collective beliefs, these are what rush out to meet any circumstance before your innate logic or reasoning can get there. Creatively intrinsic, your Midpoint beliefs are buried by decades of repetition that melt into habit, over time perfecting one of four personas of coping to gain acceptance and care. The first is to force or menace others into demonstrating care towards you, using intimidation to gain the level of care you seek. The second is to challenge, grill, question or judge another into demonstrating care towards you, constantly berating another until they concede. The third is to run away or remove yourself from the pack, forcing others to chase you, thus winning a demonstration of care through others seeking you out. The fourth is playing the victim to entice others to comfort you and take responsibility for you and your actions, playing on the heartstrings of another's compassion or empathy to elicit care.

Regardless of which of the four you internalized as your own, the mastering of a coping persona did not mean you learned to effectively cope. Drew Barrymore said, "I took the stairs and felt like my childhood took the elevator". You learned a localized model of response designed to draw out demonstrations of care. Functioning on *auto-pilot*, it plays in the background of every situation ensuring you repeat and are limited to the coping mechanisms, behaviors, patterns, judgments and opinions of your caregivers. And since all this was learned in childhood, at a time when everything is forever, that *auto-pilot* programming was barely noticed and certainly never questioned.

Take, for example, the Midpoint beliefs of 'life is hard', 'anything worth having is worth fighting for' or 'no pain no gain'. Such beliefs wreak havoc when they result in you perceiving yourself as having to suffer in some way to be worthy to receive. Such thinking motivates you to plow through adversity as a venue for building character, breeding the distrust of ease and giving way to a personal identity based on WHAT you do rather than WHO you are. By adopting such beliefs that the determination to burrow through adversity will result in you being a strong, resilient and contributing member of society, this becomes your only option for proving you are deserving of care. If your child-self concluded that what you did was not worthy of attention or care, you experienced the emotional realization that who you were was also not deserving. This adds the tempo to your personal theme song as it lingers behind your learned self-image, triggering the judgment that your strength, resiliency and contribution are less than worthy as well.

As you learned to identify yourself through ownership of Collective and Midpoint beliefs, you began to form Exclusive beliefs. Unlike Collective beliefs that are obvious and governed by society or Midpoint beliefs that taught you how to interact to gain care, Exclusive beliefs are deeply personal. Exclusive beliefs were specific to your child-self as they were based on your individual rationalization that fear will keep you safe. The extent to which you felt emotionally and physically safe as a child within your early environment, shaped your Exclusive beliefs. It determined your perceptions, interactions and influenced how you navigated the world around you. In other words, Exclusive beliefs are the result of fear, not danger.

Exclusive beliefs are not linked to tangible experience. They represent how the Collective and Midpoint are translated by an individual. Like a child who is inexplicably afraid of the dark or thinks there is a boogie man under the bed. Such beliefs are specific to your child-self but are not directly about you as a child. Exclusive beliefs frame the other beliefs and how you interpret them internally. They formed the perceptions that remain with you today.

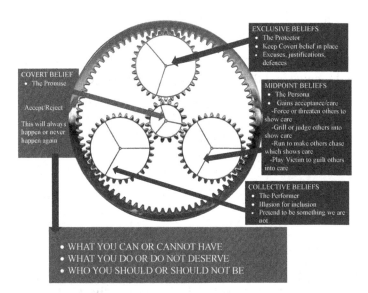

EXCLUSIVE BELIEFS
• The Protector
• Keep Covert belief in place
• Excuses, justifications, defences

COVERT BELIEF
• The Promise

Accept/Reject

This will always happen or never happen again

MIDPOINT BELIEFS
• The Persona
• Gains acceptance/care
  -Force or threaten others to show care
  -Grill or judge others into show care
  -Run to make others chase which shows care
  -Play Victim to guilt others into care

COLLECTIVE BELIEFS
• The Performer
• Illusion for inclusion
• Pretend to be something we are not

• WHAT YOU CAN OR CANNOT HAVE
• WHAT YOU DO OR DO NOT DESERVE
• WHO YOU SHOULD OR SHOULD NOT BE

Collective beliefs are like the canvas. Midpoint beliefs are frames built on circumstance and experience, while Exclusive beliefs are the chosen medium. But it is the Covert belief that is the artist. At the core of all the beliefs you hold from childhood, it is the Covert belief that paints the picture of the other beliefs within your child-self's mind. It arises from one experience at one specific moment in time. It is the Covert belief that gives consent for who you are as an individual. This is the belief you create about SELF. The Covert belief is the judge of the 'me' you perceive yourself to be.

Of all the layers of beliefs, the Covert belief is most likely to be revealed through personal language. "I can't travel alone", "Sorry I bothered you", "I'm such an idiot" and "I couldn't help it", reflecting deep-seated judgment. Your Covert belief narrates the illusion that attention, importance, value and worthiness are your only animation. It is the result of what you consent to deserve and receive and determines what you can or cannot hope for in life. This consent is given the moment a childhood promise is formed and ultimately lays the groundwork for the learned identity you use to define yourself throughout your life.

Exercise

Turn to a blank page in your journal. Draw two lines, dividing the page into three equal columns. Label the first column 'Collective beliefs,' and write five Collective beliefs that were instilled in you before the age of five. Was there a behavior that all of society would notice or reprimand you for if you continued to perform it? Was there a perceived societal consequence that frightened you into proper behavior, or an actual societal consequence that you experienced? Once finished, move to the middle column.

Label the middle column 'Midpoint beliefs', and along the top of the column, write the society label for the type of caregiver you had as a child. Use labels rather than names, such as mother, father, grandmother, uncle, dividing the Midpoint column into smaller columns for each caregiver you had. Choose one caregiver and take a few moments to consider what you learned from them, what they stood for, and the main point of influence they offered, or you learned in their presence. If you had one word to describe that caregiver, what would it be? Identify the Midpoint beliefs behind this caregiver's words and actions, what they believed in, practiced and instilled in you, either intentionally or unintentionally. For example, did this caregiver infuse your childhood with religion, music or dance? What about the words this caregiver used? Language is the most prominent indicator of Midpoint beliefs. Did you hear phrases like "What would the neighbors think?" or "Take it like a man" or "Idle hands are the devil's playground"? Was there a saying or phrase that instantly comes to mind? What was the Midpoint belief you learned from this?

Repeat this practice for each of the caregivers most prominent in your childhood.

Once you have a good sense of the Collective beliefs and the Midpoint beliefs that enveloped your early years, cover up those columns and move on to the final column. It is important that you do not look at what you previously wrote as it will pull your memory in the direction of the Midpoint beliefs or, defiantly oppose them. So, do your best to keep the previous columns covered.

Label the final column 'Exclusive beliefs' and write five Exclusive beliefs you created for yourself as a child. Remember, Exclusive beliefs are created by fear and are specific to you, but not about you. For example, did you believe there was a boogie man under the bed? Were you afraid of the dark? Did you have an imaginary friend that kept you safe? List five Exclusive beliefs you held as a child, where each came from and the fear behind it.

When that is complete, compare all three columns. Look for similarities between your Exclusive, Midpoint and Collective beliefs. Your Exclusive beliefs are a result of how you viewed yourself through the Midpoint and Collective ones. The threads that link the Midpoint and Collective beliefs to the Exclusive beliefs were crucial in building your reality as a child and thus, have become the foundation of the learned self-image you carry with you today.

Exercise

Your Covert belief like your own personal theme song, plays in the back of your mind reframing every experience to fit within its limitations. That will change right now.

Grab a pad of sticky notes and, in bold letters on each one, write out the following statement:

I value and respect myself and everyone can see it.

Put that statement on as many surfaces as you can around your home. Put it in places you will see it often, your bathroom mirror, your refrigerator, your front door. You can even carry it with you in your pocket or write it on your hand. Every time you see it, smile and read it out loud. After just one day, you will be amazed at the things that happened that you wouldn't have thought possible.

2

BELIEFS AND THE SYNTHETIC SELF

"Your childhood brought you here.
Look at it. Own it. Embrace it.
It is the artwork of your being."
-Sky Stevens

The hidden influence of a forgotten promise intricately weaves itself into every moment of your existence, restricting who you are and how you live. It reduces every choice, every experience and every thought to fit within its limitations and filters your life through the lens of a man-made version of self.

You know now that Collective beliefs are society-approved beliefs that condition you to conform through the modeling of norms, values, and acceptable conduct. Midpoint beliefs model the behaviors, patterns, judgments and opinions you inherit from your early environment's view of Collective beliefs. Exclusive beliefs represent your place within the Collective and Midpoint beliefs. But the hidden influence of a forgotten promise becomes the Covert belief that directs your personal experience while navigating all the rest.

Unlike the Collective, Midpoint and Exclusive beliefs that are learned over time, the formation of the Covert belief is instantaneous, from one experience at one specific moment in time. It is the moment a promise becomes the architect of your being. At any other stage of life, a promise pledges a specific behavior for a specific amount of time. *I will shovel the snow when I get home from work. I will do yoga every morning for a week.* In childhood, when you faced an overwhelming circumstance that left powerlessness in its wake, self-preservation took center stage, and you vowed to reclaim your personal power or live without it forever. That promise lasted a lifetime as your Covert belief.

Meet Jamie. Jamie was a three-year-old who frequently heard "You never clean your room". It was constantly referenced around the house and the punchline of daily jokes. It was laughed about with neighbors and relatives. Every time Jamie heard "You never clean your room", Jamie felt something stir inside. One day, after a grueling teasing, Jamie set to work cleaning the room to the best of the young child's ability. Jamie was proud of the effort and convinced that this would end the external torment and calm the internal one. With great determination and excitement, Jamie invited the teasing adult to view the room. The adult took one look and, in a sarcastic tone, said, "You didn't close the closet door. There is a sock under the bed. And the windowsill is filthy. Like I said, you never clean your room!" With a chuckle, the adult turned from the door and walked away. Unable to fully comprehend what just happened, Jamie flopped on the bed and punched a tiny fist into the blankets. With gritted teeth, the child uttered a statement that set the stage for the rest of their life. "I will NEVER clean my room again". And just like that, a promise was born.

Such an experience cut through to the core. If your child-self was lucky enough to have nurturing and aware caregivers to offer the tools to process such a blow, you would have worked through it and filed it away with other past experiences. If not, the emotion and the hurt joined forces, sending your psyche into a tailspin of unexplainable, unmanageable feelings, and leaving you to draw only one conclusion. This will never happen again. You made a promise to yourself that you didn't ever intend on breaking. And there it began. The construction of the fortress. Each painful experience added a new brick, each unmanageable feeling the mortar until a hint of ridicule finished it off with a new and shiny turret. Without realizing it, your true self, that beautiful individual treasure that you identified as 'me', vanished from sight, hidden deep in the recesses of your new fortress.

The promise resulted when your child-self perceived that something about you, some innate quality was defective and thus singularly responsible for causing a threat to the level of care you received. It was an instinctual decision to compromise your innate being, your Natural Self, in exchange for care. That choice began the formation of a new self-image based on how and when you perceive care, and in what way you interpret or acknowledge the care you perceive. You noted which parts of your Natural Self were acceptable and deserving of care then revised or reduced all that did not generate care. The perceived defect was hidden completely.

When this happened, it formed an inner bond that was greater than anything else because it occurred at a stage of life when everything was forever. Just as your child-self declared the toy that would be your favorite forever, the shoes you would wear forever or the food you would eat forever, so did your child-self forever give consent to accept or retaliate against the level of care you perceived as being lost because of a perceived defect in your natural way of being. In your child-self's eyes, that alleged defect compromised the receipt of the care necessary for survival. The promise was primal. With the promise came a story that solidified your definition of care, how and when you receive care, and your acknowledgment of it. The promise became your story, and the Covert belief became the narrator of that story. Every minute of every day, your Covert belief provides a never-ending commentary on the role you vowed to play based on your definition of care and your perception of your worthiness to receive it.

In Jamie's case, the Covert belief's narration tells the story that the amount of care one deserves is directly related to the cleanliness of one's bedroom. Therefore, independent of the bedroom, Jamie would not be deserving or worthy of care. The Covert belief is specific to the promise made by each child. Say, for example, a caregiver does not have the capacity to provide emotional comfort toward a child and instead provides comfort through food. The child makes a promise to self that food is care. Every time the child experiences upset, the caregiver offers a delicious morsel designed to draw the child's attention away from the upsetting situation and back toward the caregiver. The child's Covert belief narrates a story that food will comfort any upset within the child's life. Through into adulthood, the now-grown child does not trust nor recognize demonstrations of care by others. Only food is associated with care and thus secures survival. Every child, within their first five years, forms a Covert belief based on a promise made to self. Regardless of gender, culture, or environment. It just happens once, yet the belief lasts a lifetime.

The promise you made to yourself as a child occurred the moment you chose whether to compromise the care essential for survival to live in the innate Natural Self or compromise the innate Natural Self to secure or maintain the care necessary for survival. Your child-self consented to adopt this man-made, operantly modified version of yourself designed to have less, deserve less, and always be less than your Natural Self innately is. Over time, the manufactured version slowly eclipsed the Natural Self entirely, maneuvering your life onto a singular track piloted by the promise. Thus, the Synthetic Self is born.

In the first year of life, every child lives in the Natural Self. By the second year, they are deep in battle with the domestication and conditioning process that dominates their early environment, as they fight to maintain their innate Natural Self despite teachings and reprimands, scoldings and consequences. In the third or fourth year, a moment hits that backs the child's instinct into a fight or flight state resulting in a promise that alters the child's existence and transforms their life from a natural state to a synthetic one. The resulting Synthetic Self, propelled by the Covert belief, keeps the promise alive in a secret life of concealment. The Covert belief's main function is to maintain the level of care that the child perceives they deserve based on their promise. It adopts justifications, excuses, defenses and behaviors to extract care from the outside world to validate it.

Like an unforgettable melody, the Covert belief steering the Synthetic Self continues to play the silent yet powerful theme song. It is your personal soundtrack, running in the background, navigating your way through a life steered by the promise. With the promise now buried in decades of excuses and justifications, your Covert belief still tells the story of what you should and should not do, can and can not have, will and will not achieve. With the constant replaying of the self-imposed limitations of your Synthetic Self over so many years, it is now a habitual way of thinking, with the Collective, Midpoint and Exclusive beliefs modified in its wake. The longer the promise steers your life, the more familiar and habitual its programming becomes. Your Synthetic Self runs on *auto-pilot,* constantly announcing its commitment to the opinions, shame, judgments, fears, perceptions and insecurities that keep each piece of your Synthetic Self's armor in place. The longer your theme song plays, the heavier the armor of your Synthetic Self.

Jamie grows up and becomes successful, recognized and honored professionally. Jamie now lives in a big, beautiful home with house staff instructed to clean around Jamie's bedroom and respect it as Jamie's sacred space. At the end of every day, Jamie experiences a momentary hesitation at the bedroom door. A sense of unease and apprehension accompanies this brief pause before entering the room and, an odd sense of freedom when leaving it. At night, seldom, if ever, does Jamie sleep. In frustration, Jamie turns to prescription medications to trick the body into a restful state. Jamie secretly craves a personal sanctuary to re-group in at the end of the busy days but can't quite seem to achieve that end. Convinced there is never enough time and justifying that no one sees it anyway, Jamie determines to solve the bedroom issue... tomorrow.

Jamie often gets invited to the homes of colleagues for business meetings or gatherings. But as Jamie stands in the doorway of yet another colleague's meticulously organized bedroom, an unsettling weight rises from within, prompting a stream of careless remarks to escape Jamie's lips; "It's so clean, it's like no one lives here". "You probably aren't as busy as I am and have way too much time on your hands". When alone, the impromptu comments echo in Jamie's mind, conjuring a wave of guilt and shame as the sting of embarrassment collides with regret.

Your Covert belief has one purpose, and one purpose only, to restrict your functioning to the limitations of your promise. It views each of your experiences through the lens of your Synthetic Self. It determines what you deserve based on your promise and ensures you get it. Take, for example, if a person's promise revolved around a lack of money and how unworthy they were of wealth. The narration of their Covert belief would leave that person uttering, "I can't seem to get ahead financially". "Money goes out as fast as it comes in". "I can't afford that". "I'm always broke." Any time that person receives money, a big expense shows up to put them right back where they started. The theme song of their Covert belief narrates the lack of money story, while the woe-is-me lens of their Synthetic Self sees only the patterns that ensure this end.

Like most, you were conditioned to view each aspect of life separately and may not realize how influential your Covert belief is. Yet, it weaves its way into every aspect of your life. You wouldn't notice, for example, that a promise to be unworthy of wealth ensures that each time a money pattern cycles around, creativity is stagnant, energy is low and healthy eating goes out the window. The promise is your comfort zone, and your Synthetic Self enforces it. Anytime you step out of that comfort zone, it is the Synthetic Self's job to sabotage your efforts and keep your life confined within the boundaries of your childhood promise. It is a beacon that attracts the experiences, people, and energy level that further enforce the promise. With your theme song constantly playing, over time it convinces you that the profile of your Synthetic Self is who you naturally are and what you naturally deserve.

Yet, there is nothing natural about it. It is not who you are; it is simply a synthetic version of self, constructed within the boundaries of the promise. And, like most, you built your entire life within those margins. Every friendship, every job, every success, every failure, every aspect of your life functions within the confines of the promise and through your Synthetic Self.

However, the information in your child-self's hands at the time you made the promise was not valid. None of it was true. Meaning that the promise itself has no solid or legitimate foundation. Yet, your child-self, in that one moment in time, believed it all to be real. Your child-self's purity, inexperience, lack of knowledge, confusion and fear prompted it to view a threat to its receipt of care. For your child-self, it was a necessary preservation tactic. In other words, it was the level of acceptance your child-self consented to apply to what was told, taught, or learned, that set the framework for the promise, without the reasoning, information or problem-solving skills to decipher it in a realistic way.

It is not what you deserve, but what the promise dictates that keeps limitations in place and your life stuck. It is living through a Synthetic Self that is not willing to step beyond the confines of your childhood promise that restricts your current life. A promise from the past that limits your present. The Synthetic Self functions on *auto-pilot,* applying its past programming to everything in the present, enforcing all that will honor your promise.

When something new happens that the programming of your Synthetic Self cannot restrict, your Synthetic Self taps your Covert belief on the shoulder and says, 'My programming isn't working here. Do something'. The Covert belief steps in and applies a good old-fashion temper tantrum. Your Exclusive Belief reasons that your physical body is bigger now and less flexible, so kicking and screaming and throwing your body to the floor as you might have done when your body was small and more flexible will only cause undo pain and damage, so it persuades the Covert belief to apply a verbal defense instead. This typically comes out as blame, competition, justification, or defense. It is the same basic tantrum, designed for the same result of keeping the promise in place. It is just different packaging.

If you encounter someone who consistently relies on blame, shame and guilt, their Synthetic Self is at work. They redirect your attention while their Synthetic Self searches its programming for a situation that is remotely similar using shame, blame and guilt to buy it some time. When their Synthetic Self has located the limitations that apply, it can calmly reposition the conversation onto familiar footing and continue as if nothing happened. If questioned, their Synthetic Self will reframe the entire situation, positioning itself within the limitations of its programming, most typically in the victim's role. You, by this point, have grown confused and frustrated. To the one who relies on blame, shame and guilt, however, you are inexplicably 'attacking' them for no reason. Being an audience to another's Synthetic Self is frustrating especially if you feel the conversation is important, or exhausting if you repeatedly are the one to bring the conversation back to the original point, which is guaranteed to start the process all over again.

When one lives through their Synthetic Self's lens, they cannot perceive or even consider new ideas, information or different ways of doing things, often criticizing or judging those who can. Living within the Synthetic Self leaves you stuck within the framework of your promise, repeating the same patterns, attracting the same things, and achieving the same ends. For example, one oppressed as a child may meet someone in adulthood who sees potential and value in them. Their Synthetic Self would search its programming for a similar situation. Coming up empty because they have never experienced being valued before, their Synthetic Self would conclude the other person must either be mistaken or lying and deem them untrustworthy. Their Synthetic Self must make the other person wrong to keep its programming and the promise right. So, it stands firm and insults the other person for even suggesting value is present. After all, if it was true and they had value as a person, that would mean their Synthetic Self was a fraud and all the information in its programming bogus. Since their Synthetic Self does not have the programming to deal with that, it redirects the conversation, picks a fight, blames, justifies, defends or challenges so it does not have to consider the new information as a possibility.

To fully understand this concept, you must appreciate all that was happening around you at the time your promise was formed. First, you must appreciate your caregiver's role. There is no blame here toward your caregiver, for they were operating from their Synthetic Self just as you currently are, and their Synthetic Self was influenced by their caregivers, whose Synthetic Self was influenced by their caregivers and so on back through the generations, just as yours was influenced by your caregiver(s). Needless to say, your caregiver had an immense impact on your impression of you as a child. Your caregiver's level of concern for you in your early years, their interest in and attention toward you played a key role in the Synthetic Self you fashioned.

The word attention stems from the Latin *'attentio'*, which means *to attend to*. It is the term given to the frequency, duration and caliber of notice your caregiver extended to you in your early days. The moment you perceived that level of care and *attending to* to be threatened, halted or shifting in its frequency, duration and caliber, your survival instincts took over. Being too small to fight and without the resources to take flight, you adjusted the only thing you could control. You.

Take for example, a caregiver's frequency, duration and caliber of *attending to* that showed genuine interest, a child would have adopted a genuine interest in self and created a promise based on that. Yet if a caregiver typically offered a low level of *attending to*, a child would have adopted a 'less than' interest in self, having learned they were less important than other things, and used that as the foundation of their promise. In either case, if the child perceived a sudden shift in the frequency, duration and caliber of *attending to*, the result would be a reshaped sense of self designed to invite and/or maintain the level of interest they are accustomed to. For example, if a single caregiver got married, or a younger sibling was born, which severely slowed the frequency, duration and caliber of *attending to*, the child would reshape their sense of self by vowing to either accept the new identity of being invisible or to becoming the center of attention as a retaliation against it. However, if the sudden shift in frequency resulted in an increase in the level of *attending to*, someone started hovering, overshadowing the child through excessive frequency, duration and caliber, the child would reshape their sense of self to match the ineffectual existence now expected of them, and demand constant hovering from everyone. The level of interest the child learns to hold for themselves contributes to the intention, delivery and impact of their promise, which ultimately becomes the backbone of the Synthetic Self they form.

It is important to note that your child-self perceived the available level of *attending to*, then formed its Synthetic Self based on that level. It was not necessarily the level of *attending to* that was available to you at the time, merely the perception of such by your child-self which influenced your level of self interest, which prejudiced your promise that steered the Synthetic Self you created. This has all become your current perception of yourself, of your life and the world around you. If, as a child, you experienced negative attention that singled you out and sent your emotional psyche into a tailspin of epic and unmanageable proportions, you would have drawn the only conclusion possible. This will never happen again! Without an alternative, your imagination presumed the problem was you, not the environment. This is what happened with Jamie. The frequency, duration and caliber of the '*You never clean your room*' level of *attending to* by Jamie's caregiver became the foundation of Jamie's Synthetic Self. Into adulthood, it influenced Jamie's interaction with others (the cleaning staff and the colleagues who showed their bedrooms) demonstrating externally the sense of self Jamie's Synthetic Self had in place internally.

Such an experience in the first five years of life may slash, shrink or even shatter self-esteem. The child-self absorbed the information provided by a caregiver, added its own and decided instantly which part of the Natural Self was to be altered to maintain the level of *attending to* initially offered. Though your body changed as you grew into adulthood, the habitual programming of your Synthetic Self did not. It simply revised the justifications, excuses and re-directions to meet the societal expectations of each age, refining the Synthetic Self to be more suitable for a mature, adult body. Meanwhile, your promise remains safe, and your habitual thinking remains in place.

The longer you live under the reign of your childhood promise and bow to your limiting Covert belief, the longer you dishonor your true and Natural Self. When you dishonor yourself, you lead by example, mentoring others to dishonor you in the same way. Like attracts like. You may know you deserve more, but your Synthetic Self will not allow it, so you turn to the outside world for validation. You expect others to respect you when you do not respect your innate SELF, to care for you when you do not show care towards your Natural Self and to love you even when you do not love your authentic self. Even if you found all this in others, it would be your Synthetic Self they respected, cared for and loved; a man-made version of you. Though you may seek change and take steps to evoke change, with your Synthetic Self tethered to that old promise, it will never allow for permanent transformation.

Striving for change without unleashing the promise at the base of the Synthetic Self is like moving your slippers to the other side of the bed and convincing yourself you renovated. Humans have that tenancy, to slightly shift insignificant pieces of their lives, altering only what does not directly affect their Synthetic Self, and label it as *change*.

For real change to occur you must locate your promise and bring it to light. Every experience you've had and still have, is related to, resulting from, or engineered by that old promise whose boundaries, limitations, and parameters currently control your life. It is still dictating the amount of love you deserve, the amount of money you deserve, the health you deserve, and the caliber of relationships permitted for you. However, the fact that you seek change means that you have begun to outgrow your Collective, Midpoint and Exclusive beliefs. All that is left for complete transformation is to expose the promise, destroy the Covert belief and stand back while the armor of the Synthetic Self crumbles. Only this will uncover the Natural Self and the true life you were meant to live.

Exercise

Locating the promise at the base of your Covert belief takes some digging but this exercise will reveal it. Take out your journal and turn to a blank page.

<u>Step 1</u>

Down the left-hand side of the page, write a loose history of your first five years of life. Make the list as accurate as possible relying solely on your memory. Do not ask family for assistance for this practice is to reveal your child-self's perception. Leave enough space under each entry for additional information to be added later and keep the list in chronological order. Write only the facts, until your sixth birthday, then stop.

Sample Step 1:

- ***Born July 2, 1952 in Detroit, Michigan..lived at 102 Robinhood Drive in Barbarry subdivision***

- *When I was 2 years old, the family moved to Ann Arbor, Michigan*
- *At 3 years old, I started kindergarten at Bower elementary school*

<u>Step 2</u>

Under each entry, using a different color, add a sub-fact. For example, a vacation you went on, a pet that joined or left the family, or when a sibling was born. Refrain from narration or behind the scenes commentary. Just write the facts. Carry your journal with you for a few days to add memories as they show up.

Sample Step 2:

- *Born July 2, 1952 in Detroit, Michigan..lived at 102 Robinhood Drive in Barbarry subdivision*
  - my baby sister was born Aug 2, 1953

- *When I was 2 years old, the family moved to Ann Arbor Michigan*
  - got our dog 'Charlie'

- *At 3 years, I started kindergarten at Bower elementary school*
  - mom cut my hair so I was presentable for school...I liked it the old way

- *When I was 4, we had a summer vacation in Florida*

<u>Step 3</u>

Using a third color, add your personal memories, things you liked, or didn't like, and why. (Catch yourself if you attempt to embellish a memory with emotion or blame towards your child-self or others from your past.) Perhaps you flopped down on the bed and declared never to clean your room. Or you stomped outside, hid behind the shed, and started crying, determined that these things would just keep happening. Maybe you have a memory of when you sent your mother's Royal Doulton Figurine flying across the room and watched it shatter. How about when your sister pulled your hair, and you got in trouble for it? Or when you watched your dad kick your brother out of the house for smashing up the car when it was your oldest sister who did it. Embrace the memories as they come and weave them into your list.

Sample Step 3:

- **Born July 2, 1952 in Detroit, Michigan..lived at 102 Robinhood Drive in Barbarry subdivision**
    - my baby sister was born Aug 2, 1953
    - my grandmother lived with us and looked after me because both my parents worked
    - my grandmother used to give me hot chocolate even though my parents didn't allow me to have it

- **When I was 2 years old, the family moved to Ann Arbor Michigan**
    - my grandmother moved to a nursing home

- got our dog 'Charlie'
- *Charlie knocked me down when we were playing and I cut my forehead on the coffee table*
- *I stayed away from Charlie and all dogs after that*

- **At 3 years, I started school at Bower Elementary**
  - mom cut my hair so I was presentable for school…I liked it the old way
  - *the kids made fun of my hair, so I used to sneak out a hat in my pocket and put it on when I got to school*

- **At 4 years, we had a summer vacation in Florida**
  - I stepped on a jellyfish and got stung
  - *mom told me to stop crying and that challenge was the cornerstone of life, but it really hurt. I found a secret place in the trees and hid there, crying. I felt alone and abandoned and swore I would never show emotion again*

Step 4

Keep adding memories. The promise you made to yourself is there in your first five years of life. One of your memories will reveal a time when you vowed to fight against what was happening or surrender to it completely. When that critical memory shows up, sit with it. Take the time to remember the circumstances surrounding it and write it out in your journal. You may experience a

Sky Stevens

rush of emotion. Let it out in the most undignified way possible! Cry, yell, laugh, scream. Just go with it. It is a release of the emotion you have been harboring for years, so let it out.

PART II

WHAT BELIEFS CREATE

Synthetic Self

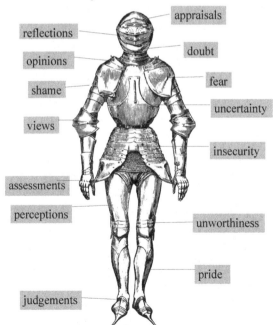

appraisals

reflections

doubt

opinions

fear

shame

uncertainty

views

insecurity

assessments

perceptions

unworthiness

pride

judgements

3

BEHIND THE SCENES OF
THE SYNTHETIC SELF

*"One's ability to grow and change
stems from a willingness to see
their effect, existence or character"*
-Sky Stevens

Living in your Synthetic Self is like wearing a suit of armor. It may feel like a protective shield, but really it is a facade that hides your innate light under a label of 'damaged goods'. Beneath the heavy armor of your Synthetic Self lies a treasure trove of learned practices that, over time, have fallen into habit. By exploring the intricacies of your Synthetic Self's internal structure, you gain greater insight into its programming and a deeper understanding of how and why it has such control over your present life.

The internal structure of your Synthetic Self works like a machine. Just as a toaster toasts bread and a coffee maker makes coffee, the single task of the machine-like Synthetic Self is to translate the parameters of the promise into tangible experience. To do this, your Synthetic Self must first identify what your experience is, and then how to squeeze that experience into the confines of the promise. If the experience reaches beyond the comfort zone of your promise, it is your Synthetic Self's job to rein it back in. This process, often labeled insecurity or low self-esteem, is really your Synthetic Self's functioning, ensuring it places the limitations of your promise over every encounter you have.

Just as the toaster kicks into action each time you push down the handle, your Synthetic Self kicks into action every time a new person, environment, or circumstance shows up in your life. It scans each to establish if the experience is as your promise allows by comparing itself to the outside world. Its radar is constantly assessing. Do you appear better or worse, healthier or sicker, smarter or dumber, wealthier or poorer, more attractive or less attractive, fatter or slimmer, taller or shorter, more successful or less successful than everyone else? The more comparisons it makes, the more threats it perceives, the more fear it creates, the more defensive it gets. Such is the complex world of the Synthetic Self and the reason for the 'seeking state' you find yourself in today, seeking care, seeking attention, seeking validation, and seeking proof of your worthiness.

If you keep yourself living comfortably within the promise, the Synthetic Self can rest. If, however, you dare to step beyond that comfort zone, with the mildest thought that you might be more, the button on your Synthetic Self gets pushed and it springs into action.

Your Synthetic Self keeps your adrenals on overdrive and your body in dis-ease. Unlike your Natural Self, your Synthetic Self is not organically fed. It survives on validation and never gets enough, which leaves your body fidgety, impatient, and in constant motion, moving awkwardly under the armor that immobilizes your current life. It is the old emotion that weighs you down as you struggle to keep your place on the emotional poverty line dictated by your promise. Each piece of the armor is a sensitivity of your child-self that was locked in place as assessment, appraisal, perception, opinion, view, reflection, and judgement. Each of these sensitivities resulted in the shame, pride, fear, uncertainty, insecurity, unworthiness and doubt that make up the rest of the emotional armor of the Synthetic Self. The combination keeps your child-self accepting responsibility for the frequency, duration, and caliber of the care you receive, even now.

To your child-self, care was more than survival, more than the provision of food, water, shelter, and space. It was a comparable measurement of attention, importance, value, and worth. It is still seeking care in the form of belonging.

Though each person's Synthetic Self is unique, the underlying programming is derailing the good, and sabotaging circumstances and situations to keep you living down to the promise you made. It causes you to throw your hands up and wonder why you just can't seem to catch a break. It asks others to honor you, respect you, embrace and accept you. Yet all the while you feel fraudulent because you know you should be honoring, respecting, embracing and accepting your truth. Deep inside you know your truth and that you were made for more, but your Synthetic Self will never allow such truth to surface. So, you shove the responsibility in another's lap, hoping they will see how great you are and give you permission to have and be everything you want without you having to betray your promise.

While you wait for that fraudulent feeling to subside, you bury yourself in the alleged security of the Collective beliefs model of relationships, teaming up with another for guidance, companionship, attention, affection, decision-making, finances, responsibility and yes, validation. Collectively, you achieve financial stability, buy a house in the suburbs, reproduce, accumulate and consume. You buy and display all that reflects inclusion and conformity of neighborhood and community. Yet, your Synthetic Self's radar continues to scan the horizon. The moment it detects a lack of interest or care; it perceives the averseness as a threat to its alleged security, resulting in an aggressive fear-based reaction.

Fear is the knowing that you have gambled your truth (Natural Self) for a measurable value and worth (Synthetic Self) and lost. Fear, like beauty, is in the beholder's eye. No other living soul can know the fear of your unreasonable, illogical, and irrationally formed Synthetic Self because your child-self's perception of a threat to care was what formed it. Fear is an individual plight defined by eyes that have something to lose. Your Synthetic Self experiences fear on some level every day though not seen, tasted, smelled, or even identified within. Your Natural Self's instincts can only detect danger (being chased by a saber-tooth tiger, for instance) and danger has a simple outcome; only one survives.

Unfortunately, the instincts of your Natural Self have been long overshadowed by your Synthetic Self's reaction to each perceived threat. You either run away from the perceived threat with shame or guilt, or run towards that threat with defensiveness, aggression, or blame. The power you gave to your Synthetic Self in childhood, has long since reprogrammed the adrenals to perceive a physical threat where an emotional threat of exposure is present. It sounds off the alarm and sends your body into battle. Thus, your body suffers under the perceptions, expectations, observations and translations of your Synthetic Self. For it senses great fear where your adrenals would not typically detect danger.

Much different from danger, fear is an emotional response that spreads through the Synthetic Self unnoticed, for it is the backbone of its programming. Fear is the single most powerful force that can motivate any human form. Fear alters the perceptions of a child, placing a thorn where everyone else can see a rose, and fear continues that perception into adulthood. Programmed long ago, your Synthetic Self still panics when it perceives a thorn, even when no physical harm is present; in arguments, in blame, in judgment, in the wake of brutal honesty and especially in the assessment of your Synthetic Self itself.

A Google search for the definition of fear reveals that fear is "an unpleasant emotion caused by the belief that someone or something is dangerous, likely to cause pain or a threat." Where your Synthetic Self is concerned, it isn't a person or event that creates fear, but your Synthetic Self's perception that something or someone will expose its fraudulent design. Your Synthetic Self is an illusion on high alert, afraid of getting caught, of being exposed, constantly defensive and on edge. Fear is the very foundation of your Synthetic Self for it was formed by a promise based on fear. Without fear, you would live freely in your Natural Self.

Your Natural Self is the knowing of your SELF based on your innate truth. Your Synthetic Self is a learned self-image based on a childhood fear. If your Synthetic Self dominates, you will react to each illusion of fear as though it were a real threat to attention, importance, value, and worthiness. That fear will keep you hidden in disgrace or send you roaring out into the world with both guns blazing. It will dress you in the latest fashions or commit you to the same haircut for 30 years. It will fill you with resentment or lay you in the shadows of shame. It will drive you to superhuman strength or paralyze you completely. Fear is a powerful force. The fear of not being good enough, smart enough, or worthy enough sits at the base of your Synthetic Self and sabotages your dreams.

It shines like a beacon on a lighthouse calling to all who would take refuge in your apprehension. It flashes out into the world and attracts all that is drawn to its light. Like a moth to flame, the people, circumstance, finance and opportunity that keep your fear in place come for refuge, mirroring your Synthetic Self's fear back to you through life.

According to Merriam-Webster, a mirror is "a piece of glass that reflects images". However, a mirror is also "something that shows what another thing is like in a very clear and accurate way". Thus, life, "the ability to grow, change" shows you what you are like in a very clear and accurate way, offering you an opportunity to put that growth and change in place. Your Synthetic Self will limp into victim mode once it perceives a detrimental ambush of bad luck from each person, circumstance, finance and opportunity. You stand at the mercy of life as your Synthetic Self persistently evaluates its effect, existence and character and measures itself by life's declaration of its worthiness to exist. But you have a choice. You can view your life through the eyes of that learned self-image or through your innate truth. Through your Synthetic Self you will always perceive life as a reflection of you and live in fear that you cannot or will not measure up.

A reflection, according to Merriam-Webster, is "something that shows the effect, existence, or character of something else". The lens through which your Synthetic Self views the world sees life this way. As something that shows the effect, existence, or character of you. It views life as personal. Yet, there is another point of view to consider. A shift of perspective views the reflection as displaying your Synthetic Self back to you so you can see it in a clear and accurate way. While fear shines from your Synthetic Self like a beacon on a lighthouse, it is a great opportunity to view what you are putting out in the world in a very clear and accurate way. It can inspire you to look at how you show up through the eyes of your innate SELF. All that is required is the willingness to look at your life this way. The words you choose, the way you live, and the relationships you build, are reflections, displaying the effect your Synthetic Self has, the existence it has created for you and how it defines your character.

As a machine operating a programmed system of response, your Synthetic Self extends its programming to every person and situation and attracts the same back. It is not personal. It is simply what is attracted to the beacon of your Synthetic Self. Your Synthetic Self perceives someone stealing from you as a direct stab against you, robbing you of some vital piece that defines you. But through this new perspective, someone stealing from you is a sign that you are robbing yourself in some way. The closer you look at yourself, the more your life expands because the closer you look, the more you see. The more you see, the more you release and resolve. The more you release and resolve, the less limited your life is and the more expansive it becomes.

Meet Kit. One day, a fellow Kit knew from the past called to say he was coming into town and wanted to visit.

They hadn't seen each other in a long time, and Kit was excited by the visit and felt honored to be on the fellow's short list of people to see during his limited time in town. On the day of the visit, however, the fellow called to say that something important had come up and he had to cancel.

Kit felt embarrassed and humiliated, kicked to the curb as miniscule and less than. With emotions running rampant, the *auto-pilot* response of the Synthetic Self kicked in, turning the situation into a mirror of self-worth, solidifying the injustice and allowing the delicate nudge of resentment to edge its way into Kit's mind. To avoid being seen in this way, Kit put on a 'good sport' mask and responded with a low, melodic "Oh no that's ok." Acting nonchalant as if it didn't matter. As soon as the call ended, however, Kit immediately called a friend to lash out and badmouth the fellow for canceling, hoping in vain this friend would agree with how victimized Kit was. The longer the tirade, the more the resentment festered, building a grudge that catalogued all the character flaws this fellow had displayed over the years that Kit had known him.

When that call ended, Kit felt unsatisfied and unsettled. With a journal in hand and a pen scribbling violently, Kit's emotions exploded on the page. Exhausted, Kit sat back and questioned if life was displaying a reflection. "Do I treat people like this? Do I make plans and cancel when something better comes along? Do I rate people by importance and callously discard the less important when someone more important requests my presence?" Kit employed brutal honesty and realized that it had happened. Kit's Synthetic Self reassured that it had been done with proper notice and only when it was necessary. After all, Kit did not randomly discard others, and truly honored the commitments Kit made, so what was this situation trying to say? Kit decided to go deeper.

This fellow's actions demonstrated that (a) Kit was disposable (b) Kit was less important to him than whatever came up and possibly (c) with a choice between Kit and the other situation or person, Kit was the one who would be easily cast aside without consequence. Was this true? Did Kit allow SELF to be dishonored and still wait patiently on the sidelines until the dishonoring person sought Kit out again? By telling this fellow it was ok to treat Kit this way, was Kit absolving him of all responsibility and allowing Kit to be the consolation prize?

It was gut-wrenching for Kit to discover that 'yes' was the truthful answer to these questions. With more digging, it was revealed that Kit's Synthetic Self really did (a) allow Kit to be disposable (b) make Kit step back without causing a scene, and agree that what came up was, is or must be more important than Kit and (c) allow others to dishonor Kit while Kit sucked it up under the justification that any friendship was better than no friends at all. It was all true. This fellow was simply treating Kit the way Kit's Synthetic Self did. Kit also realized that harboring anger and resentment toward someone who was mirroring the way Kit treated self, was like smashing a mirror, hoping it would change the way Kit looked. Or, as Nelson Mandela had put it, "Resentment is like taking poison and waiting for the other person to die".

So, Kit then asked some difficult questions about the way Kit showed up in life. 'When did this become my life? Where had such a belief about my unworthiness come from?' Kit searched back into the past for some clues. Clearly, an underlying belief lay unresolved. Methodically, Kit recapped past friendships and relationships, even employment. Though Kit was determined to distinguish this situation as an isolated incident, Kit uncovered a lifelong pattern of stepping aside for important people that led back to childhood.

In Kit's early life, having a voice was one thing. Being heard, however, was determined by how loud, needy, or demanding one was. Kit was a shy kid and often was shoved aside when passions took over. When and if Kit attempted to voice an opinion or need, others interrupted, talked over or drowned Kit out. They talked over each other, over the radio and the television, and the loudest and most dramatic voice won the race. The squeaky wheel got the proverbial oil.

There it was. Kit had been shoved aside. Kit lacked the theatrical expression necessary to compete, making a promise that the 'back burner' was Kit's rightful place behind the important people, until Kit barely existed at all. Kit had vowed to be benched like the rookie player, quietly sitting on the sidelines while the star players did their thing. Only when and if the important people were through, was Kit invited in. With this new insight, Kit's feelings of resentment and being victimized by this fellow's actions slowly faded. Kit now understood that Kit had attracted people who mirrored Kit back to self, assuming Kit would happily step aside and be content at the back of the line.

Kit called the fellow back, determined to take ownership, and saying it out loud was a good place to start. It was time to set the record straight. Kit was no longer willing to be treated this way by Kit's Synthetic Self or anyone else. It was time to stop playing second.

Now, some folks, upon hearing of a friend's moment of clarity, may be supportive and encouraging, respecting their friend's growth, asking questions and showing genuine interest for their friend's highest good. This fellow was not one of them. His Synthetic Self took Kit's declaration as a direct stab against him. He got defensive and slammed down the phone. Though Kit's admittance offered a safe place for the fellow to question and explore his own beliefs and behavior, he wanted none of it. This was, to Kit, a clear sign that he was not a true friend, but a messenger and teacher who showed up to assist Kit in learning an important lesson. Kit did not hear from him again. However, because of this situation and uncovering that old promise, Kit began to monitor each word, thought and action to ensure Kit honored self always and was now content to walk away from anyone or anything that dishonored Kit in any way.

As an adult, you do not still ride the same bicycle you

rode when you were three years old, play with the same toys or wear the same clothes. Yet, left in the Synthetic Self's hands, you squeeze your adult-self into the old belief and promise you had back then. Your sense of self has grown around the promise like a plant around a trellis and still uses the promise as its framework. It is separate from who you innately are and once you step back to objectively observe your Synthetic Self, you can witness it in action.

Your Synthetic Self shows up in your wardrobe, personal hygiene practices, diet and health. It shows up in the eyes and body language. It shows up through idioms, slang, self-deprecating remarks, expressions, boasting and relentless monologues. But the most obvious indication of your Synthetic Self's presence in your life is in language. The words *should, always* and *never* are absolute anchors to your promise. Your language supports your Synthetic Self's justifications, excuses and re-directions, showing up in phrases like 'I *should* do that', 'I *always* do it this way' or 'I could *never* accomplish that'. Such phrases work like affirmations, further committing you to the programming of your Synthetic Self. No matter what you do for a living or how much money you make, the language cultivated around your promise, acts as the prominent descriptor of your Synthetic Self. Being conscious of how and when you use the words *should, always* and *never,* in everyday language, will uncover the trellis used to keep your self-imposed limitations in place. The more you repeat these words, the stronger your acceptance to those limitations. There are exercises in the back of this chapter to unveil how and when the words *should, always* and *never* show up in your everyday language and uncover your promise from the past, the trellis used to keep it in place and the self-imposed limitations that curb your present life.

Remember, your Synthetic Self is a man-made beacon for care. *Should, always and never* baits others into demonstrating care towards you. The Synthetic Self does not recognize genuine care, like a fish that swims right into your hand. No. Your Synthetic Self baits the fish with language used as a worm, rod and reel, positioning you as a victim, at the mercy of the unseen. *'I could never do it. I'm always the shortest. But you are so much taller, I bet you could do it'*. It preys on the compassion and sympathy of others to sustain it. Unfortunately, the language you use as bait is often more successful than you realize. When your Synthetic Self describes a situation as *'a pain in the neck,'* it will attract a true neck injury for you. When it complains *'I'm sick and tired of this'*, you get sick shortly thereafter.

Your promise restricts your Synthetic Self to the lens of the child who created it. It perceives and describes itself through a child's eyes, as broken or damaged. *'I'm always broke. I'm too old. I am such a loser. How could I have been so stupid? Don't listen to me'*. It will also exaggerate its current state. Saying, *'I'm freezing,'* when you have a slight chill or, *'I mangled my hand,'* when you get a paper cut. And like the child who created it, it uses baby talk to describe itself. *'My tummy hurts. I have an owie on my finger'*. It will talk non-stop as it feeds on validation, incapable of breaking the stream of attention once it has one. It will meet another's concern with a five-minute monologue from its only reference point, your past, leaving everyone in its wake as 'less than' and feeling elevated by default. It will also say '*yes*' to things you don't want and '*no*' to things you do, keeping you locked within the boundaries and limitations of the promise. If these tactics don't work in a particular circumstance, your Synthetic Self simply does more of it harder. Like the person who pushes the elevator or crosswalk button repeatedly, your Synthetic Self creates intense and sometimes hostile reactions when faced with the transparency of its fraudulence to gain a desired level of attention.

Such intense and hostile reactions work to redirect others away from seeing all your Synthetic Self wishes to hide and towards its adopted banner of damaged goods, ensuring you live down to your Synthetic Self's learned self-image. But you can shift your perspective. You can consciously choose to look closely at yourself and consider that life always reflects your internal mindset. It is up to you whether you use the information life offers as a mallet to hammer yourself into the ground or as a teacher to lift yourself up and out of what no longer serves you.

Exercise

In your journal, start recording when the words *should*, *always* and *never* come up in your language. When you catch yourself using any of these, consider the whole statement a reflection of that old promise. Ask family, friends, and co-workers to point out when you speak one of these words. Distinguishing individual words within your speech may be challenging, but others will delight in pointing them out, so only ask people you trust to have your best interest at heart. After five days, you will have a list of sentences that include *should*, *always* and *never*, revealing the exact areas of your life your Synthetic Self is most prominent.

Give yourself permission to apply brutal honesty to this exercise, it will uncover much about your promise from the past. Sift through your list and identify how and when you describe yourself as broken or damaged, exaggerate your current state, use baby talk to describe yourself, talk non-stop, unable to break the stream of attention coming to you, say *yes* to things you don't want and *no* to things you do, monologue about your past, or leave others as 'less than' in your wake.

Then, consider each statement in your list. Do they accurately describe you in the present? Write yes or no beside each one. There is a knowing, a voice deep inside that distinguishes true from false. Using *should, always* or *never* does not accurately describe who you truly are, only the person you have agreed to be as your Synthetic Self. By ensuring your language accurately reflects who you are, you match the inside with the outside and steer yourself toward an authentic life.

4

LIFE IN THE SYNTHETIC SELF

*"Each of us holds a proficiency of SELF
that allows for the rendering of good.
Ownership is the only falter."*
-Sky Stevens

Embrace your Synthetic Self as a teacher. It reveals the truth of how you currently view and interact with yourself. Likewise, the life you have built reveals how you currently show up in the world. It will never lie. The truth it reveals may seem daunting, but it is the only path to freedom. Without viewing your Synthetic Self in a clear and accurate way, you will remain blind. And though you may not feel ready to witness it, it provides a reference point on which you can measure change as it comes.

To recap, your life mirrors your promise. A mirror is literal. It displays what you are doing. Life is literal too. It displays who you promised yourself you would be. The amount of love you promised you'd receive, the amount of money you promised you'd earn, the quality of health and relationships you promised you'd have. Life as a reflection clearly and accurately reveals your Synthetic Self and allows the promise and beliefs to be viewed objectively. Thoreau said, "It is not what you look at that matters it's what you see." The nose is too big, the arms are too fat, the legs are too short, and the eyes are too close together. This is what the Synthetic Self sees, but not what another person is looking at. Embracing the reflection of your Synthetic Self unveils the dis-ease within. Reflections always have something to teach and regardless of what life reflects, it will consistently display how you perceive yourself in the present moment. As your perception shifts, so does your life. The more willing you are to witness the truth about what you created long ago and take ownership of it, the more your life will expand. The more genuine and authentic you become, the more genuine the people and situations you attract.

When you live in your Synthetic Self and meet another person living in their Synthetic Self, the Synthetic Selves use each other for validation, creating a co-dependence. You find the other person so comfortable to be around, so familiar, you feel you have returned to the home of your past. That is exactly what you have done. The familiarity is so strong and the comfort you experience is so enticing you would follow the other person anywhere. And follow you do, right down the wrong path. Instead of the blind leading the blind, it's the stuck staying stuck, with the stuck. It is a reflection screaming to be noticed, not true love blossoming. If you are not paying attention, your old beliefs may find you hopelessly turning a teacher/student dynamic into a movie-like romance.

Teachers show up when the student is ready. When you are open to learning without judgment, you will embrace the teachers when they come. It's like signing up for a class. If, for example, you signed up for a Spanish class, would you demand to review the lesson plan before you agreed to take the class? Probably not. You would decide you wanted to learn Spanish and commit to the course, trusting in the teacher and accepting the lesson plan as the teacher presented it. The same goes for life. If you decide you want a richer, fuller, more deliberate life, sign up and trust the teachers who come and the lessons they present and that all of it is for your highest good. As you learn more about yourself, you may, without even knowing it, reflect another person back to themselves and inspire great learning for them.

Teachers show up at random times, but typically when you question yourself the most, like a gentle reflection from the Universe to test your conviction. Welcome the teachers that reflect your Synthetic Self back to you. Each one of them will most definitely get your hackles up but if you are open to the opportunities to grow and challenge your beliefs, your defenses will fade.

The Universe is incredibly patient. It knows how thick your Synthetic Self's armor is. So, it offers you many lessons, through different teachers and different circumstances, until you learn the lesson that releases a piece of your Synthetic Self's armor. Sometimes you will require the proverbial brick wall to fall. Sometimes you will get it the first time around. Sometimes you will recognize a piece of your Synthetic Self in hindsight after you have had time to process.

View every person and every situation as a teacher. Your Synthetic Self repeats the same patterns over and over, so the teachers and lessons repeat just as often until you finally hear the wake-up call and start looking within. It is time to open your eyes and look around your life, at the people, relationships, and environments that shape this chapter of your existence. What have you attracted? Does your world seem to flow naturally? Or are there constant bumps and hiccups along the way? Have you chosen to place yourself in the audience, on hold, while others perform for your undivided attention? Do you clamor for the spotlight? Are you intrigued by the greatest potential of your highest good? Do you risk being seen in all your glory? Do you hide behind someone else's? Are you healthy, happy, and at ease? Are you unhealthy, unhappy, at dis-ease?

To see the teachers as they come, you must take a step back. You must play observer in your own life. Even amid hackle raising, arguments, or unwelcome circumstance, ask how you can be true to yourself in that moment and a teacher will appear. Do not judge. A teacher will show up when you are ready to be a student. You need only be open to it. Judging yourself or others simply puts your life back within the limitations of your promise, keeping you stuck and prohibiting your growth. So, trust every teacher that shows up. They grant you an opportunity to identify the habitual thinking of your Synthetic Self so you can break free to a new way of living that serves your highest and truest SELF.

You have the capability to come clean with your past, to choose what to keep and what to let go of and move forward, fully engaged in living. Locked in old beliefs and ideals, you can be alive for fifty years without truly living one single moment of it. Question everything you think, feel, and say. It will be one less minute you haven't lived. Release the control of your Synthetic Self and accept what comes. Commit to a new mindset, even if you don't know what that is. Just commit to the possibility of a new way of being and let your life flow in that direction. Control is the Synthetic Self's mastery. When you stop trying to control every aspect of your life, your life will flow naturally.

Do not, however, discount the speckled companionship that has graced your life thus far, for each has been a teacher. Each was a stepping stone that led you to this moment. A past relationship that appeared hurtful and heartbreaking at the time taught you discernment. Being falsely accused by another's Synthetic Self's defenses taught you to be more tolerant. A disappointment taught you to go in a direction you had never considered before. That speckled companionship of your past, whether it be a relationship, career move, roadblock or emotion, has brought you to this moment. Acknowledge them, then let them go.

The most influential of the speckled companionship of your past is shame. That painful feeling of humiliation

---

is a big part of your Synthetic Self's armor today. Justified for so long, your Synthetic Self wears shame like an accessory, weighing you down, projecting out, and inviting more shame in. You probably don't talk about shame, never mind admitting to the experience of it. But it is there. Silently, you have built your adult life around it, displaying yourself to the world as one of shame's children, thus attracting a shame-full life. It is important to note here that shame is not something you created for yourself. Shame is like a basketball thrust into the hands of a vulnerable child, and your child-self was conditioned to accept it.

Understanding the shame embedded in your Synthetic Self is important because it is critical to understanding that the shame was, and always has been, the property of the person who imposed it. Not of the child who received it. It was never personal, though it is a valuable tool for understanding the makeup of your Synthetic Self. Whether or not you can identify and name the shame you hold, you can return it to its rightful owner. And you can do it with grace. Though it may sound unjust and unrealistic, even silly, to return a perceived infraction against you with grace and honor, it will lighten your load immensely. The very act will dislodge a piece of your Synthetic Self's armor and remove the trigger from ever being activated again. For your life to shift, you must return shame as a gift. Consciously and with honorable intent from your Natural Self.

To return shame as a gift, you must address the card

56

to the Natural Self of the shame's rightful owner, even if you don't know who that is, and frankly, it doesn't matter. The only way for you to be liberated is to return shame honorably. Your Synthetic Self, if charged with the task, will do the opposite, thrusting shame back to its rightful owner with a vengeance as payback, keeping its patterns alive, and re-creating the cycle that attracts more shame into your life. It will invest your time, attention and energy in replaying the infraction, fueling and reaffirming its power over you and your life and putting a magnet in place to attract more shame for you to invest more valuable time, attention and energy in.

Shame has become so much of your Synthetic Self's identity that it moves through your present life unnoticed. It is placed in your hands by anyone, at any time and from anywhere, especially from your Synthetic Self where it is used to keep you small. When you are functioning in the *auto-pilot* programming of your Synthetic Self, your hands are open to accept shame even when it comes from within. Though it may sound horrifying to admit or identify shame within yourself, it is liberating. It allows for the understanding and acceptance of your worth and value.

Meet Anna. Throughout her life, Anna repeatedly stated, "I never have enough money". It was her theme song. She talked about it constantly and believed it accurately described her. Anna cut coupons and bought only what was on sale. She'd think long and hard about what she truly wanted, then go out and buy the closest thing she could find for the cheapest price. One day, Anna's girlfriends were visiting while Anna sorted through her closet. Anna pulled out a black tank top from just inside the closet door. It was brand new and hung perfectly on the hanger. She turned to her friends and said, "Does anyone want this? I will never wear it." Her friends took one look at Anna and laughed. Not privy to the joke, Anna's hackles began to rise. One friend patted Anna's shoulder and said, "Go look in the mirror." With her friend's gentle hand on Anna's back, Anna walked over to the full-length mirror and looked. Staring back at her was a woman in an old black tank top that was ripped along the neckline and stretched out of shape from years of wear. Her friend smiled and said, "Do you realize you give away new things and keep the old, worn-out things for yourself? You do it all the time." Anna stared at her reflection as her friend offered examples around Anna's home.

Anna defended herself to her friends, insisting she was being noble and selfless. That it was an intentional fashion statement. She justified she supported recycling and was doing her best to lessen the landfill and protect the Earth from a disposable society. But as she spoke, Anna looked at the evidence around her home and, for the first time, really saw it. The truth was right in front of her. She wasn't cutting costs; she knew what she wanted and settled for less. She had a new tank top in her closet, hidden from sight, while she justified wearing the old ripped one. Anna had been depriving herself, living a self-imposed Cinderella story. She had made a promise as a small child that she was 'less than'. She deserved less and could only have less. She had been keeping herself locked in shame, small, living down to her child-self's promise ever since. Anna sank to the floor as uncontrollable sobs released decades of shame. When the sobs subsided, Anna stood. She pushed her shoulders back and her chin up. Proudly, she retracted the offer to her friends and changed into the new tank top, putting the old one in the 'get rid of' pile.

Change is the natural order of things. Winter changes into spring, the night changes into day, and caterpillars change into butterflies. Releasing shame evokes great change. Humans are not exempt from change. Your Synthetic Self merely resists it. Resistance, like shame, can cripple both the mind and the body. You can resist the idea that you are living with shame and be ashamed of your resistance. This is how the Synthetic Self digs in its heels and keeps you in its grasp. It retaliates against and sabotages change. Yet, as the tadpole changes into the frog, great transformation can take place in human life. You must learn to trust the highest version of your Highest Self (the Natural Self) and go through the process to complete the transformation. Imagine if the caterpillar resisted metamorphosis. Dug in its heels and revolted against becoming a butterfly. This is what your Synthetic Self does. It keeps you from being a butterfly. The resistance and shame lodged in the Synthetic Self is not a natural part of life. Yet, change is. Change affects the world in a positive way, while shame and resistance infect it.

You cannot do both. You cannot affect your life in a positive way and allow your Synthetic Self to infect it at the same time. When your Synthetic Self infects, it contaminates, discredits, and dishonors your life and the lives of those around you. Your life reflects that infection. But you can positively affect the world by dismantling your Synthetic Self's armor and letting each piece of your Natural Self shine through. When you affect the world, you make a difference. You have a positive impact on your life and the lives around you and life reflects that positive back. Those in ease, naturally affect. They grow, change, evolve and mentor those around them. They pay attention, take ownership and strip their Synthetic Self down, discarding the old, stale beliefs that serve no purpose but to hinder their 'coming out' in their highest glory. Affecting the world views life as a series of teachable moments. Each one invites an opportunity to learn about your Synthetic Self and release it. When you are ready to unshackle yourself from your past and be the person you truly are, you see a reflection that reveals the effect, existence, and character you are opting for. In short, you affect your life.

You can consciously choose to affect the world by exposing your Natural Self or infect it by continuing to allow your Synthetic Self's armor to plow through your life like the proverbial bull in a china shop. Each person must choose for themselves. Male, female, young, old, married, single, kids, no kids, it doesn't matter. You alone commit to living in your Natural Self. No parent, spouse, friend, child or sibling can assist with this. By playing the role of observer in your life, you will clearly see where you stand in that commitment and whether you are currently affecting or infecting. It will be instantly visible by your reaction to the teachers when they show up. You will either immediately retaliate with *No, I don't* or absorb the learning with *Do I really?*. When you react to life's teachers with *No, I don't* you infect; contaminating, discrediting, and dishonoring your life and the lives of those around you. When you react to life's teachers with *Do I really?* you affect your life. You open yourself up for transformation, embracing the lessons life offers as a gift. The one you choose keeps you locked in either your Synthetic Self or your Natural Self.

Meet Geri. As a small child, Geri visited regularly with an esteemed uncle. One day, this favorite uncle sneezed, then jokingly said he must be allergic to Geri. Geri, being a small child, took the comment literally. Instantly, shame resulted. Geri reasoned that a favorite and cherished uncle would not lie. On *auto-pilot*, the adult Geri flinched every time someone sneezed. If the person was in proximity, Geri would leap from the sneezing person, justifying that stepping back was to avoid germs.

One day, Geri and a friend were walking down a crowded sidewalk when a man walking in the opposite direction sneezed as he went by. Geri's friend offered a 'gesundheit' and smiled to the gentleman, then turned back to find Geri on the road. The friend pointed out Geri's unusual reaction to sneezing. Because Geri had no memory of the original event with the uncle, Geri immediately became defensive. Geri's Synthetic Self harbored an unidentifiable belief that Geri caused others to sneeze, which triggered shame every time someone sneezed near Geri. Geri was, of course, unaware of the shame that anchored Geri's Synthetic Self. However, a trusted friend stated this, so instead of lashing out, Geri considered response options.

It is in such moments that "the ability to grow and change is to be shown your effect, existence or character" truly comes into play. Geri, like anyone else tangled in the web of shame, has two options. Geri can react to the trusted friend with either *No, I don't* (Synthetic Self) or respond with *Do I really?* (Natural Self). Geri can allow the *auto-pilot* of the Synthetic Self to lash out or consciously choose to embrace the feedback to unveil an old promise that is steering Geri's life.

The *No, I don't* reaction is your Synthetic Self's armor stepping out to protect the promise, and thus the alleged defect from being seen. It is defensive and pointed. It implies an outsider has intentionally plotted against what you have created and all you have kept hidden. *No, I don't* is the Synthetic Self's first line of defense. Re-directing another's attention so you can remain comfortably under the radar. It projects the shame of the Synthetic Self out into the world with resistance and accusation, shutting down any chance of exposure, growth, or learning.

No, I don't is a coverup, plain and simple. It is a neon sign that broadcasts you function in your Synthetic Self and have no interest in yourself beyond that initial programming. When life presents a teacher (in this case, the friend's message), your Synthetic Self comes out swinging, using *No, I don't* as a weapon with which to kill the messenger. In essence, you are blind to the message while shooting the messenger. Such verbal posturing offers you only fight or flight as a next course of action.

The *Do I really?* response is an open stance for learning and feedback. Life offers a reflection that results in growth and personal freedom when you honor both the message and the messenger. It invites the other person, who is expressing interest and demonstrating care, into your world as a teacher. It is an opportunity to recognize shame. *Do I really?* opens you up to ask, "How can I be true to myself in this moment?". It invites you to identify your Synthetic Self's tired habits and embrace every opportunity for your Natural Self to take center stage. With every *Do I really?* response, another piece of armor crumbles, exposing more of the Natural Self. The *Do I really?* response guides you further on the path toward living fully in your truth.

On the path to your Natural Self, judgment and excuses fall away. You can be grateful to your child-self for protecting you and doing everything in its power to invite care. Then you can tell your child-self that you can take it from here. As an adult, you have the power to restore your life to one that reflects and honors the complete, radiant, and unlimited being your Natural Self innately is. By releasing the old promise and having all the beliefs that were built on that promise released as well, you are now free to choose the life you want. To become a butterfly. To help with the process, you can employ a mantra that states, "I now live in my highest SELF and release all that does not serve my highest SELF." Remember Jamie from Chapter 2? Jamie employed such a mantra to counter the *'You never clean your room'* identifier Jamie used since childhood and a week later, Jamie de-cluttered and re-arranged the bedroom and slept happily ever after.

Exercise

It is time to return shame. This exercise requires consistency, five minutes twice a day, for five days. Even if you don't think you carry shame, do this practice for shame lurks in the muscles and cell memory where you can't see it.

First, find a quiet place where you can be alone uninterrupted and stand in the middle of that space. Next, close your eyes and inhale. On the exhale, speak these words out loud:

"I return the shame to sender. I apologize for holding on to it for so long. I now present it to you as a gift and, with gratitude, I step boldly into my highest SELF."

Visualize putting shame in a box and wrapping it with paper and ribbon, then lifting it and handing it back to a faceless, nameless and genderless silhouette. Refrain from attaching any identification to the sender.

Take a deep breath in and exhale through your mouth, blowing the shame out of your body and releasing any emotional ties to it. Repeat this inhale/exhale exercise for five minutes every morning and every evening for five days. At the end of the five days, you will feel lighter and stronger and will notice a shift in your world. Change is inevitable, and you are ready for it.

Exercise

Across the top of a new page in your journal, use a pencil to write the names of five people whom you respect, value and enjoy. They could be colleagues, siblings, teachers, grandparents, or even someone you don't know well but admire. Under each name, list the reasons you respect, value and enjoy them. You may include how you feel when you are in their presence and what about them makes you feel that way. Take your time with this to ensure the list is accurate and complete.

When the list is as honest as you can make it, erase the people's names. You now have a list of the qualities, values and activities that you respect, value and enjoy. Attach the list to the bathroom mirror or the refrigerator, somewhere you can view it multiple times a day. Then go about your day implementing those qualities, values and activities. You will be re-training your brain to treat yourself with respect, value yourself and enjoy functioning from the highest version of you.

PART III

THE ROAD MAP FOR CHANGE

5

REDEFINING SELF THROUGH THE SCOPE OF CONCERN PYRAMID

"The only one who sees fit to cast judgment at the beginning of a journey, is the one who inspires not to finish it."
-Sky Stevens

As a youngster, your child-self learned that its level of self interest came from another's eyes. When asked what you wanted to be when you grew up, you learned to align your answer with the level of achievement, status, or preference of those outside of you. They rejoiced if you expressed interest in being a fireman. And celebrated if you dreamed of being a veterinarian or ballerina. However, what would have happened if your child-self expressed an interest in becoming all that it could be or exploring all it was capable of? If your child-self looked your caregiver straight in the eye and openly declared that when you grew up, you would step beyond the status quo, be true to yourself and seek your true potential, living in the highest version of your highest good. What reaction would have followed? Even within the most loving of families, the reaction would have been something like, "That's great, but how are you going to pay your bills"?

Like most, your initial conditioning taught you to value another's opinion over your own. To shift your life, you must do the opposite. You must prioritize what you think of yourself and ignore what others think about you. The level of interest you have in the highest version of SELF decides what you think about your abilities, potential, and capabilities. When you direct your interest in that way, you expand the level of concern you hold for SELF, and this is the key to transformation. It alone contributes to or takes away from the fullness and richness of your life.

Concern is not conceit or arrogance. It is not pride or vanity. In fact, it is quite different. It is what determines your quality of life. Your Synthetic Self requires a low level of concern for SELF to keep its limiting beliefs in place, while your Natural Self enjoys an expansive level of concern for SELF to embrace all the possibilities for your life. When you intentionally elevate the level of concern you hold for SELF, it puts the promise, and the beliefs built from it, in perspective and destroys the power they hold.

Concern and attention go hand in hand. One cannot exist without the other. Concern engages your interest and care. Concern for SELF engages your interest in and care towards SELF. Your attention locates the exact point in time and space in which you place concern. This means attention can be consciously and actively set. It is the most important thing to understand about attention. You can choose what to *attend to*, and offer interest and care to, in every moment. Remember, the Synthetic Self, like the promise, performs behind the scenes as your personal theme song. On *auto-pilot*, it hijacks your attention, placing your focus on what keeps its limitations in place. To release yourself from the Synthetic Self's power, you must be cognizant of what is happening within. You must consciously choose what to focus your attention on and thus what to offer your interest and care to. In other words, you must notice what you notice.

To notice what you notice is a real skill, one that few people tap into. It is rare amongst the status quo where most simply get through; get through the bills, get through the meals, get through the workday, get through the week. Yet with all the 'getting through', how often do you tune your attention, interest, or care towards yourself in a sincere and meaningful way? Instead, your Synthetic Self's programming moves you along on *auto-pilot*, *attending to* the job, *attending to* the house, *attending to* the accumulation of money and riches, *attending to* Facebook and *attending* to the next oil change appointment in the Smartphone calendar. Instead of investing in SELF, the Covert belief uses your *attending to,* to create an image, story or performance designed to secure the attention of others, not the attention of the highest version of you. You scan the horizon for someone or something to marvel at, the blond, the brunette, the sports car, the big house. You even marvel at the person who is marveling at you. Yet can you recall the last time you truly marveled at yourself?

When you are ready to stop the cycle of patterns that keep your Covert belief in place and invite a new way of being into your life, you need only notice the *attending to* patterns that have steered your life thus far. This simple practice will estrange you from the life you've known, a life steered by the Synthetic Self, and allow instinct, intuition, and the innate wisdom of the Natural Self to take the reins. After all, these are the qualities that truly distinguish one person from another. To embrace these, you dare to shatter the self-imposed limitations that promise inclusion and form an unbreakable alliance with the unique qualities that set you apart. The only way to do this is to pay attention to how you pay attention.

The Scope of Concern Pyramid™ maps this journey. It tracks the path from the lowest level of *attending to* yourself, the Synthetic Self, which keeps the limiting beliefs in place, to the highest level of *attending to* yourself, the Natural Self, which allows instinct, intuition, and innate wisdom to steer your life. The fact that you, as a child, believed what you learned about yourself and agreed that another's opinion of you was more important than your own makes the Scope of Concern Pyramid™ possible. With a conscious and deliberate interest in SELF, you develop a level of reasoning that opens the possibilities and potential for your life.

The Scope of Concern Pyramid™ explores the relationship between reasoning (how you think about SELF), self interest (the level you *attend to* SELF) and the resulting level of concern (how much consideration and care you offer to SELF). The Scope of Concern Pyramid™ demonstrates that when self interest shifts, the level of concern for SELF shifts as well. Likewise, when reasoning shifts, the level of self interest and concern shift too. Reasoning, self interest and concern are the anchors of your Covert belief, promise and resulting Synthetic Self. By *attending to* yourself in a conscious and deliberate way, the power over your life returns to you. You may move up the Pyramid by expanding your *attending to* until you reach the sixth level. By this level of self interest, your reasoning is expansive, with an increased level of concern for yourself and others. At this level, beliefs no longer steer your life, your Natural Self does. The Scope of Concern Pyramid™ maps the Self Un-Covery™ process.

So far in this book, you have identified the promise you made long ago, your Covert belief and Synthetic Self, that results in your current level of self interest. (If you are still unsure of your current level of self interest, visit the exercise in the back of this chapter.) Now you can transition through the two primary manners of reasoning, the Microspective and the Macrospective, laid out in the Scope of Concern Pyramid™. To fully live in your Natural Self, you may transition through the levels of self interest in each. The generic behaviors or actions laid out as examples for each level are not carved in stone. They are simply a guideline. As you work your way up the Scope of Concern Pyramid™, your individual sense of SELF will build. You will shed layers of doubt and fear, breaking free from limiting beliefs and illuminating the path to your true potential. Those new to the Self Un-Covery™ process will typically begin

Sky Stevens

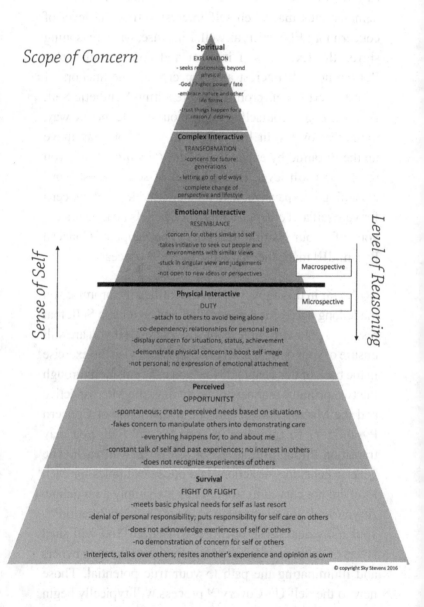

Scope of Concern

Spiritual
EXPLANATION
- seeks relationships beyond physical
- God / higher power / fate
- embrace nature and other life forms
- trust things happen for a reason / destiny

Complex Interactive
TRANSFORMATION
- concern for future generations
- letting go of old ways
- complete change of perspective and lifestyle

Emotional Interactive
RESEMBLANCE
- concern for others similar to self
- takes initiative to seek out people and environments with similar views
- stuck in singular view and judgements
- not open to new ideas or perspectives

Macrospective

Microspective

Physical Interactive
DUTY
- attach to others to avoid being alone
- co-dependency; relationships for personal gain
- display concern for situations, status, achievement
- demonstrate physical concern to boost self image
- not personal; no expression of emotional attachment

Perceived
OPPORTUNITST
- spontaneous; create perceived needs based on situations
- fakes concern to manipulate others into demonstrating care
- everything happens for, to and about me
- constant talk of self and past experiences; no interest in others
- does not recognize experiences of others

Survival
FIGHT OR FLIGHT
- meets basic physical needs for self as last resort
- denial of personal responsibility; puts responsibility for self care on others
- does not acknowledge exeriences of self or others
- no demonstration of concern for self or others
- interjects, talks over others; resites another's experience and opinion as own

Sense of Self

Level of Reasoning

© copyright Sky Stevens 2016

at the base of the Scope of Concern Pyramid™ within the Microspective reasoning. But your precise starting place is based on your current level of self interest.

Within the Microspective reasoning, you learn that limiting beliefs were assembled by a child's perception of the frequency, duration and caliber of *attending to* they received in their first five years of life. This perception was groomed by the agenda of the caregiver's Synthetic Self, not by the needs of the child. As a result, the child experienced inclusion only when on the receiving end of the caregiver's agenda. Being conditioned through another's agenda, the Microspective child built a Synthetic Self with a level of reasoning that extended well below what their personal experience could offer them.

Microspective children struggle with, and recoil from, the accusation of perpetuating or interrupting another's agenda. They learn they are a burden, often feeling unseen, unwanted and unloved. With little or no platform for self-development, the child's lack of value and importance becomes the foundation of the Synthetic Self they create and the core of the Covert belief. Their early experience teaches that the attention they receive, whether positive or negative, benefits another's hidden agenda. In other words, the attention they receive is not personal. Thus, Microspectives become suspicious of affirmative behaviors, unable to recognize or receive genuine demonstrations of care or *attending to.* Redirection and avoidance as conditioned coping mechanisms enable Microspectives to stay locked into the undeserving treatment plan. When faced with the opportunity to be more than conditioning allows, Microspectives get tangled in a victim persona, constantly seeking a buffer to hide behind, a champion to take responsibility for them and/ or move them forward. Their undeserving beliefs do not allow for moving themselves forward and thus betraying the promise they made long ago. Microspectives are typically reactive, seldom, if ever proactive. Their words do not match their actions because they secretly know they are betraying SELF. They clash with those who appear confident and self-assured.

If the typical Microspective witnessed a child falling off a bicycle, they would shut down, using justifications and excuses to postpone action until someone else stepped in, then blame that person for hijacking the situation when they were just about to act. If no one else came to help, the Microspective person might approach the fallen child, so they didn't look like a bad person by not stepping in. The Microspective then would attach an experience to the fallen child, dictating a quick outcome so they themselves could get back under the radar. "You were riding too fast. Well, I fell off a bike when I was your age and I was ok, so you are not hurt." Microspectives are quite primitive in their reasoning and react to all situations in the same way, rather than to specific individuals or experiences.

When Microspectives are ready to arrest the old patterns of the Synthetic Self and question the Collective and Midpoint beliefs they hold, they can evoke an amazing change in their life. As this happens, the level of concern toward SELF and others expands, elevating the level of reasoning to Macrospective, in the top half of the Scope of Concern Pyramid™. Here, one realizes they alone are repeating the old patterns of the promise and consciously stop to explore and analyze the Exclusive and Covert beliefs they hold. They learn to take a bigger look at the culture, environment and circumstance of this lifetime, and consider these as an opportunity to learn the lessons they are here to learn and continue their growth. They come to understand that they are not responsible for the actions of others, now or from their past. The Macrospective can rise because they no longer let old beliefs define them and consciously explore who they are in the present. If others choose to continue with the old patterns or dynamics, fair enough, but within the Macrospective reasoning, one makes conscious decisions for their own life, independent of others, and trusts the results will be for their highest and greatest good, thus the greatest good of anyone who crosses their path. It is here one begins to rise out of the Synthetic Self, consciously discarding the pieces that no longer serve the person they now are.

Macrospectives are intrigued by the world and marvel at the workings of their own mind. They become fascinated by their capabilities and curious about their potential. They consciously and graciously observe their own life, refining and defining their awareness as they move forward. They have mastered their survival and work towards understanding the promise they created and the resulting Synthetic Self and how these influence their life. They take responsibility for their words and actions.

They pride themselves on consciously ensuring to always stay in their truth by saying what they mean and meaning what they say as they work towards an authentic life. They are now aware of when and how they get drawn back into old patterns and are eager to identify those triggers.

Macrospectives are fascinated by varying points of view, exchanging ideas, and seeking other perspectives to learn and grow from. They accept each person has their own experience and their own path to follow, and that each is solely responsible for how they show up in this life. They understand each must face the effects of their thoughts and actions. They have learned that rescuing others is a detriment to the greater learning of that individual's path and the Macrospective does not interfere. The Macrospective knows their only responsibility is to the highest version of their highest SELF and consciously choose to gear their words and actions to reflect this.

More importantly, they learn no one can hurt their feelings, or wound their ego, without their consent. They know to keep their power to wound, which they previously offered to others, with them always. They are no longer willing to give their power away. If emotions stir, the Macrospective searches inward for the trigger, rather than outward in blame. They look for win/win solutions that are inclusive, considering all parties involved. They have evolved into big picture thinkers.

If the Macrospective person witnessed a child falling off a bicycle, they would rush to the child's side. They would ask a series of questions, collecting information from the child to determine the child's experience. "Are you hurt? Can you get up on your own?" They would listen and assess the situation based on the information they received from the child, recognizing this is the child's experience and they are there to assist only. "Would you like some help? What kind of help do you need?" They put the onus on the child to guide the child's experience. Only if the child could not guide their own care (unconscious or in shock, for example) would the Macrospective person take over, relying on their own experience, skill base or knowledge to do what is in the best interest of the child.

There are three levels of SELF interest within each of the Microspective and the Macrospective reasoning areas. At the base of the Scope of Concern Pyramid ™, is the Survival level with the minimum of Microspective reasoning and *attending to* oneself. Frequently alienated and/or emotionally abandoned by another's agenda and viewed as an accessory to the caregiver, those at the Survival level are in survival mode. They made an internal promise that no one is looking out for them so they must take charge of their own survival needs. At a very young age, they learn a higher-than-average level of problem-solving for survival's sake and employ it for self-preservation. They learn to safeguard themselves by reading their environment, picking up detailed clues to lessen the impact of emotional or physical threats. All information received is to, for or about surviving, and the beliefs they form hold them to this promise.

Those at the Survival level are perpetually looking

for someone to 'adopt' them, advocate for them and lead them to safety. Therefore, it is not uncommon for those at the Survival level to use phrases like "I only did this because you did that..." or "I was just reacting to you" or "You made me do it". In this way, when judgment comes, they have a human shield to act as a buffer between them and any accusation.

Those living at the Survival level are masters of illusion. Their persona is fight or flight. Fight or flight is no longer an instinct, but a way of interacting and living. These folks are like magicians performing a sleight-of-hand. Using an illusion of hardship, they distract others, while behind the scenes, they forage to get their own needs met. Their beliefs are based on pretending to be something they are not as a lure to getting what they need. Since they have little of their true selves to attract others to their lives, they use emotional hardship to bait others into taking responsibility for them or showing care towards them. They target those they judge as vulnerable and keep those people engaged by playing on their guilt, sense of obligation, compassion, or oppression. They announce a hardship they perceive for another person and lure that person in by pledging a much-needed cure. Once the person is hooked, the Survival person flips the switch. Inexplicably, the Survival person suddenly has more hardship than the other person, and with a strategic application of guilt, the Survival person maneuvers the other person into taking responsibility for the Survival person's care.

There is little logic or reasoning present at this level and truth has little bearing. At the Survival level, one uses others to get their survival needs met. Some are content with one beneficial person, while others at the Survival level may camouflage themselves with an entire decoy life, mimicking the opinions, expressions and experiences of the people within it, and even adopting another's history as their own. They imitate demonstrations of care and appease those around them by saying what is necessary to keep the decoy life and its people in place. There is no emotional attachment or loyalty to the decoy life or the people within it.

Cloaked behind the decoy life, those at the Survival level then create an alternate life behind the scenes; secretly meeting their own needs under the radar. It is not uncommon for these folks to have a secret residence, hidden relationship or concealed bank account that no one from their decoy life knows about. Once the alternate life is exposed or the Survival person confronted, the Survival person puts the onus on the members of the decoy life by affixing blame, while the Survival person quietly slips away to resume their fervent search for the next person to sustain them.

At the Survival level, the Synthetic Self believes it has no impact on the world, therefore, natural consequences are not acknowledged. These folks do not experience remorse or regret. They often set themselves up to be exposed to ensure others berate them, which reassures their promise that others will always treat them this way.

However, the constant self-deprecation and juggling of deceptions slowly eats away at the Survival person until they eat away at themselves. They chew on their hair, bite their fingernails, pick at scabs and other self-destructive behaviors to measure down to what they have promised themselves they deserve. They may even physically hurt themselves and blame someone else for attacking them. At the Survival level, everything happens to, for and about me. The Synthetic Self does not rest, and the Covert belief is playing every minute of every day.

As a result, emotions and focus move as quickly as the body as these folks vehemently measure themselves against the world. They come across as highly competitive, when, in truth, they are competing against the clock. When they see an opportunity to have their survival secured, they take it, regardless of what they leave in their wake. No matter how much reassurance one person gives them they will constantly seek the next source of validation. On *auto-pilot*, very little of what they say or do is genuine or authentic. How could it be? They have a Covert belief that they are nothing more than an accessory to others and have learned to use it to their advantage.

The next level of Self interest in Microspective reasoning is the Perceived. Here folks can manage their own basic needs and, unlike the Survival level, can experience emotion, though the expression of such can be quite deceiving. At the Perceived level, folks are semi-conscious of their behavior and mildly aware of their talents and abilities, but as their conditioning dictates, out-witting another to do something for them is much easier than doing it themselves. Hovered over as children by caregivers, the Perceived learned to use redirection to outsmart their caregiver, manipulating the caregiver into completing tasks originally assigned to the child. Unfortunately, this left the Perceived with a Covert belief that boasts a false sense of superiority. They embrace opportunities to scrounge off others, not out of necessity, but to conserve their energy and resources. Over time, the need for new and craftier ways to outmaneuver others becomes a habit that results in languid reasoning. The Synthetic Self, and thus the Covert belief, are stuck in a *minimum effort for maximum gain* mode. The Perceived creates perceived needs on a situation-to-situation basis, increasing the complexity of their tactics to manipulate others into doing what the Perceived is quite capable of doing for themselves. As with the Survival level, such tactics are not conscious.

The persona here is the Opportunist. They offer whatever is in their possession, but only if the cost is less than the return. They shower others with the illusion of concern and extend what looks like kindness, yet the intent is to receive something greater in return. And they keep score! In short, they create parasite/host relationships and are constantly on the lookout for hosts. The reasoning here is more sophisticated than the Survival level, who seeks to get their needs met. The Perceived meets their needs yet seeks to prove intelligence. Always on the lookout for the next opportunity to confirm their adequacy, they move from one person to the next like a train with many stops, collecting victories as they go.

Should another catch on, and challenge them, the Perceived simply up their game. It is not uncommon to hear phrases like "Everyone else does it for me" or "No one else has a problem with it, but you", from these folks. The Perceived talk non-stop about their past (never the present) and seldom, if ever, ask about others. They are conscious of their choices and secretly feel like a fraud for not living up to their potential, yet continually manufacture justifications or perceived roadblocks to explain why they don't.

The third and highest level of Self interest in Microspective reasoning is the Physical Interactive. With more advanced reasoning than the Survival or Perceived levels, where the focus is to get away from or get away with, the Physical Interactive's focus is to go toward. Conditioned to make a name for themselves by work-driven caregivers, and thus secure an identity worthy of care, they hold a Covert belief that a person does not exist until they are recognized by society. The Physical Interactive persona is duty. They show the level of concern relevant for the role or image they seek. The programming of the Synthetic Self is to perfect an image, even if the image is an illusion and not honest or real. Image is everything and the Physical Interactive will stop at nothing to ensure the outside world is convinced.

The Physical Interactive person is aware of their emotions and feelings, though they seldom acknowledge or express them unless it improves their image. Emotions are therefore stuffed to the point of festering and explode without warning. The Physical Interactive's concern for society's approval is the venue for validation and thus, results in co-dependent relationships that increase status. Relationships are not personal; they are business. They marry someone who is advantageous to their status when society deems an appropriate dating period has passed. Then, when society says it's time to have children, they have them. Whether they want them or would make a good parent, is irrelevant. Nothing is personal; wants and desires do not play a role in satiating the Synthetic Self's drive to impress. The Physical Interactives are not capable of genuine demonstrations of care. They show only the care necessary to the role or image they are trying to achieve, and only when outsiders are watching.

What happens behind closed doors can be quite a different story. Since the outside world does not require emotional expression or intimacy to secure one's image, there is little need for these behind the scenes. Child interaction, like all relationships, is business. The caregiver rewards the child when they contribute to the caregiver's positive image. The reward is material, also promoting the image of the Physical Interactive. Seldom, if ever, is the child rewarded with warmth or affection. If, however, the child does not contribute to the Physical Interactive's image, or provides some detriment to it, the resulting punishment, resentment and anger may last a lifetime. From the Physical Interactive you might hear "What would the neighbors think?", "Don't ruin the family name" or "If you do that, people will think I am a bad parent or person". Everything in one's life at this level (house, car, children, friends, career) secures a specific image.

In Microspective reasoning, the Survival, Perceived and Physical Interactive assume they are receiving a specific treatment from life. Life happens to them. At the Survival level, one places the responsibility for oneself in another's lap. At the Perceived level, one manipulates others into taking over the Perceived's responsibilities. And, at the Physical Interactive, society alone is responsible for them. When one owns up to their Covert belief, admits to their Synthetic Self, and questions the logic that led to these, they may transition into Macrospective reasoning. A few will find this path for themselves. A few will find awareness and responsibility through trauma or unexpected life circumstances. Most, however, will remain in the comfort of Microspective reasoning, repeating the same patterns, attracting the same events and blaming life for treating them that way.

The first level of Self interest in Macrospective reasoning is the Emotional Interactive in which the initial glimpse of the Natural Self is witnessed. Here, the subconscious becomes conscious. At the Emotional Interactive level, one is willing. They begin to acknowledge and challenge the Synthetic Self and, thus, experience the first expressions of genuine concern for SELF. Their persona is Resemblance. New to building healthy relationships, the Emotional Interactive begins by finding connection with others who have similar ideas, similar lifestyles or ways of seeing the world, and who can introduce new concepts within the tried-and-true framework. They interact with others without pretense or agenda. This is the first step to expanding concern and offering fragments of the Natural Self to the world. The Emotional Interactive compares new information to their original conditioning and, through recognition, the armor of the Synthetic Self starts to weaken.

The second and more advanced level of Self interest within Macrospective reasoning is the Complex Interactive which has transformation as the key. The Complex Interactive are curious about themselves, their abilities and potential and take responsibility for exploring SELF on multiple levels. Here, one rarely experiences the Synthetic Self. Yet, on a rare occasion that threatens the deep-rooted Covert belief, the Synthetic Self may still kick in. However, the Complex Interactive is now able to consciously summon the Natural Self to take the reins, so the Synthetic Self is quickly silenced. The reasoning and interest in SELF expands to reveal multiple facets of awareness through which the Complex Interactive addresses the parts of the Synthetic Self that still linger. Relationships are now built on multiple levels on which one can consciously support their growth and actively contribute to the growth of others. Deliberate decisions made with conscious effort observe and dissolve old patterns and beliefs and expose deep-rooted triggers. Here, one emerges from the past, with a change of perspective and lifestyle. One operating at the Complex Interactive level explores the options for contributing to the world through a positive legacy.

In the Spiritual and final Macrospective level, one actively seeks explanation and broadens their scope to allow for relationships seen and unseen. Exploration is the key. One relies on their instincts while big picture thinking is explored. At this level, one marvels at all that affects the human spirit. The Spiritual person recognizes the existence of energy between all living things and honors all forms of life. Trust is instrumental as one expands the concept of SELF to explore a greater purpose for being. With this re-framed trust in SELF and an expanded level of reasoning, one now embraces their knowing, intuition and instincts while demonstrating genuine concern for SELF and others. Grace and kindness are conscious acts, and gratitude is the new state of mind.

The Scope of Concern Pyramid™ puts the promise, Covert belief and Synthetic Self in perspective and shows you how to destroy the power they hold. When you use reasoning to take an active interest in SELF, the level of concern for SELF expands and sends a new vibration into the world that acts as a beacon for attracting a vibrant life. By *attending* to yourself in a conscious way, you move up the Pyramid and experience a stunning transformation that redefines you. Now you can deliberately set your *attending to* towards living in the highest version of your highest SELF, loosening the power of your Synthetic Self, releasing control and allowing your Natural Self to lead you on the path to an extraordinary life.

Exercise

Step 1: Think for a moment about the activities you enjoy. It could be stamp collecting, gardening, calligraphy, painting, cooking; activities through which you are actively engaging the body and mind in a creative process. Take out your journal and write the names of the activities you enjoy along the top of a blank page. Underneath each, list what you like about that activity and why you do it. Give yourself a few days to add to the list to make it as complete as possible.

Step 2: Find a photo of you when you were five years old and paste it on the same page as the list.

Step 3: Cross out the name of each activity and replace each with the word 'me'.

Step 4: Using the new label of 'me' read down each list. The reasons you enjoy the activity are the new reasons you enjoy SELF. These describe your interest in SELF and why. As you do this, note the points that you react to either physically or emotionally and use colored markers to write the reactions down beside the list.

Step 5: Once you are finished, consider the following:

What sensation did you experience turning your passion toward yourself?

How did it feel describing yourself as you described something you love?

Did it feel comfortable or uncomfortable?

Did you feel light, inspired and excited by the exercise? Or did you feel heavy, taxed, or frustrated?

Did you have to fight the urge to rip up the list? Did you rip it up?

Did the list accurately describe the ways you show concern, interest, or *attend to* SELF?

Did you abandon the exercise, finding something suddenly more pressing and more important to do, putting as much distance as possible between you and your truth?

If you justified walking away from the exercise because it took you to the edge of your comfort zone, just remember, your comfort zone was laid out by your promise. By abandoning the list, you abandoned yourself in the process. Is your Synthetic Self still playing out an old pattern of self-abandonment from childhood?

PART IV

CREATING A LIFE
BEYOND BELIEF

PART IV

6

LEARNING TO LIVE IN THE NATURAL SELF

"It is time to reclaim ALL of who I am"
-Sky Stevens

You want to speak your truth, yet often, you go head-to-head with the fear of owning all your strength. All your radiance. All your innate wisdom and knowledge. You want to speak your truth, to drop all the pretense and act from your Natural Self, but the idea of taking responsibility for your power is overwhelming. Yet, it is time. You are incredibly unique. You have a gift to share with the world and you have been hiding it the shadows for far too long.

Society places enormous importance on conformity, aesthetics, and recognition. Is it any wonder you wander around, afraid to fully express yourself? Here's the funny part. The people you fear will ridicule you or not accept your truth, are also walking around fearing ridicule and seeking acceptance from others. They are also afraid to step into their power. Which means you seek acceptance from someone seeking acceptance. You are afraid of the reaction of someone equally afraid. It is time to take responsibility for your SELF and live life feeling good. So, hold on to the people and experiences that feel good and let go of the rest. Take that bold step into your truth. Reclaim your power and live the life you are here to live!

Your purpose in this life is to expand and open yourself to living in your Natural Self. Without changing a thing, you have a brilliance unlike anyone else. You have a gift that no one else has. You have a way of thinking and doing and being that is unique to you. You have abundant energy. You have the knowing and wisdom to guide your life and you are well on your way. The only thing that steers you off course is when you allow that pesky Synthetic Self to take the wheel.

You don't need to know where you are going, to set out on the journey to your Natural Self. All you need is trust. To trust the path that is right for you, even if you don't know where it leads. To trust in your gift, even if you don't know what it is. To trust in the highest version of SELF and permit it to steer you. To trust that wherever you end up, and whatever happens, it will be for your highest good.

Yes, bills need paying, the lawn needs cutting, and other chores still need doing, yet with the expansive perspective of your Natural Self, such elements of life are minimal compared to bringing your gift to the world. "Great idea", you say "But how?"

Imagine for the moment that there are two levels of SELF. A Lower Self, and a Higher Self. The Lower Self is where fear, anger, insecurity, frustration, judgment, and unworthiness reside. In the Lower Self, you scan the horizon of life, barely distinguishing the days, hours, and minutes. The moments just pass. Clouded by information, decisions, noise, and sensory overload, you zip through your days, taking in very little of your life. Everything moves so fast that you've set your radar to scan only for that which directly affects you. You surf through phone calls, emails, and social media posts and tune out all that is not to, for, and about you. You have become immune to what feels good in your heart and are oblivious to the response of your body. In the Lower Self, you are numbed by complacency. Zipping through life with your eyes on what is coming, what you can guard yourself from, how you can avoid or side-step altercation, why things are happening to you and what you have done to deserve what shows up.

If you are in pursuit of something meaningful, the option of viewing the world as expansive is right there for the taking. Switching your perspective to see it is a whole different matter. For it takes great determination to silence your Lower Self and allow your Higher Self to take over. You just have to give yourself time to make the switch. To do this, you must slow the moments down, shift gears and consciously invite your Higher Self in.

The Higher Self is where all your strength, radiance,

innate wisdom, and knowledge reside. It allows for the possibilities of your life. It is the part of you that does not require the physical body and views your life from a bigger perspective. In the bigger picture, the world and its mix of people and events are opportunities to learn, grow and be a mentor. From the Higher Self you release your tight grip on life, let go of control, and enjoy each step along your life's natural course. You marvel at the journey and laugh at your humanness. Living from your Higher Self, like mastering any new skill, requires practice.

From your Higher Self, you can see everything clearly, and you can embrace it all. You may think guidance only comes from outside forces like angels, spirits, God, Buddha, or following a regimented religion or faith. But it does not. These are great shepherds for those who wish to follow, but they cannot guide you in Self Un- Covery. That must come from within. The inner guidance from your Higher Self offers everything from answers to direction. It allows you to see your life through a new lens. Suddenly, those who cross your path are introducing a new perspective. Events or opportunities that seem to come out of nowhere shift your tunnel vision into a new direction for living. People who go on and on about themselves suddenly become messengers. A billboard, magazine or book unveils the answer to a question. An animal, a song, or an overheard conversation present insight. From the Higher Self, guidance is available from everywhere, from anyone, from anything. All you have to do is read the signposts.

When you observe situations and events as signposts along your path and trust the message, you open yourself to the possibilities for your life. Some signposts may prove you are on the right path. Others may hint that you have taken a scenic detour. Others still confirm you're headed in the wrong direction completely. When you view each experience as a signpost, a marker to show your direction, you will move forward with ease.

Another step along your journey to your Higher Self is learning to ask questions. Information bombards you daily, leaving little time to look up and take in the sights. By asking questions, each moment becomes an experience. If you frame 80% of your verbal ramblings as questions, your world will attract a multitude of possibilities you didn't know existed. In any situation or circumstance, you can ask to be shown all the possibilities or how it can get even better or what else is out there that you haven't thought of, and your world will open. If you think about it, you have only one mind, one perspective, and are riddled with childhood biases and conditioning, which limits your thinking to your present state. You cannot possibly know all the possibilities available to you. You can only see the options listed by your conditioning and experience and pick from that select few. A few minutes every day of living in the question is all it takes to open yourself up to seeing the bigger picture of your Higher Self.

The trick in asking questions is learning to ask the right ones. If you don't, your conditioning will provide answers on your behalf. Your Lower Self, with all its limitations, beliefs, and old promise, will chime in before you are even aware of it. So, by asking, 'Why is this happening to me?' your Lower Self will conjure up every excuse and justification set through its programming and hold you and the question hostage in these. It will position you as the victim, the betrayed, the sufferer, the wounded, and pummel you right back into the hole it has built. Starting each question with the word 'what' will prevent the engagement of your Lower Self. 'What am I not seeing that is standing in the way of me moving forward?' 'What would it take for this pain to subside?' 'What would it take to shift this blockage?' or 'What else is possible?'. Asking questions of this nature invites all possibilities, uninfluenced by the limitations of your Lower Self.

A question that begins with 'what' is open-ended. It invites the impossible to be possible. If you ask, 'How can I make more money?', your Lower Self will automatically answer, 'Get a second job or work more hours or ask your boss for a raise.' Your experience, perspective and conditioning will consider all the programming it has for how you can make more money and discount any option for finding money on the street or winning a lottery or uncovering a buried treasure because these do not involve you making the money you get, and you asked specifically how you could make more money. So, be sure to ask questions that your old programming cannot sabotage, like, 'What other ways can money flow into my life?' The answer will come as something you would not have thought of.

Use your time and energy consciously. Experiences shaped by an investment of time and energy can pave the journey to your Higher Self. So, pay attention to how and when you invest your time and energy. Do you use them wisely? To be still? To cherish yourself and others? To be grateful? In the past, when your Lower Self got your hackles up, you rehashed, justified, defended and replayed the event long after it was over. You brooded for days, imagining all the things you could have said or should have done that would have changed the outcome or put another person in their place. You spent your time and energy wondering what would make another person say or do such a thing. A week later, you were still talking about it, still harboring the event in your mind, still giving it power and energy. You lost sleep over it, didn't eat over it, ate too much over it, and put your life on hold over it.

Instead, pay attention to how long it takes for such an event to occur. This is the time and energy you should invest. Nothing more. For example, if an event took two minutes to happen, give it two minutes of your time and energy. If you have an altercation with someone that lasts for five minutes, give it five minutes of your time and energy and move on. Your time and energy are precious. They represent valuable moments of your life that you cannot get back. You must invest them wisely. When you invest more time and energy in an event than it took for the event to occur, you are stealing precious time and energy from yourself that you cannot ever get back. You are reaffirming your Synthetic Self's programming that you deserve less time and energy than the event, are less important than the situation or person in the event and are okay with giving your time and energy to them rather than to yourself.

Therefore, you must retrain your brain to focus on the message of the event, not the messenger. When you invest in the messenger, you allow your time, energy and valuable moments of your life to be pulled in all directions, leaving you exhausted and depleted. If you catch yourself replaying some interaction over and over, simply tell your Lower Self to STOP! Tell it to step aside and invite your Higher Self to take the reins, thus curbing your time and reclaiming your energy and directing it back to you for your highest good. This keeps your energy close to you, where you can use it to grow, learn, and shift yourself into all that you can be. Living in the full potential of your Highest Self is the greatest gift you can offer to the world.

Another step along the road to living in your Higher Self is to make conscious decisions. Decide what you want and learn to ask for it. Do not ask for what you don't want. To those of you who take this statement as a declaration of the obvious, it is time to look closer. By making choices based on what you don't want, you create a life with the remnants that remain. Your life becomes the consolation prize. "I don't want them to be mad at me for doing this, so I will do that". The process of elimination steers your life. You may think you decide based on what you want, but your language says otherwise; "I don't want that to happen, so I will do this".

It is time to give your truth more consideration than

your fear. Which means giving it the spotlight by taking the time to assess your needs and wants and honoring them. Do not deceive yourself. Lashing out at someone because they can't read your mind or won't take responsibility for you getting what you want, is not in your highest good. Hurtful actions and words stem from fear and fear alone. Recognize your reaction to fear. Do not draw others into your fear (the whole 'misery likes company' concept). You can choose to stand tall and allow your words to reflect the highest version of you. So go ahead. Make a decision that honors your Highest Self and respect it enough to say it out loud.

Another step along the journey toward your Higher Self is to listen to your body. Consider for a moment how you would draw the human body. You would sketch the body proportional to the head, the height of eight head lengths. Which means the head is one-eighth of the body. So why do you put so much stalk into what happens in your mind and ignore the rest of your body?

When you question yourself or believe things about you that are not true, your body lets you know. Emotion is experienced, recognized, and stored in the body. The emotion/body connection goes back as far as time, through vast cultures throughout the world and shows up in language. You get 'butterflies in your stomach', 'shivers down your spine', 'cold feet', 'gut feelings,' and 'a broken heart'. You 'wear your heart on your sleeve', 'bite off more than you can chew', 'see eye to eye' and 'keep your chin up'. There is a reason these common phrases suggest an emotional component to your body. Yet, still, you only listen to the mindless chatter of the Lower Self.

Your mind chatters incessantly, while your body bellows from the rooftop. Your mind tells you to do one thing, while your gut says something else. To live in the truth of your Higher Self you must listen to your body. Your mind turns ideas into reality through your physical body. Millions of inventions prove this, and you use these inventions every day. You, too, have created something with your hands that started as an idea. Perhaps it was a painting, a wood-carved chair, or a beautiful garden. You can't help but marvel at the creativity of the human mind. However, the human mind can also have ideas that are detrimental to the body, trapping emotion in the organs and dis-ease in the joints.

The voice of your Lower Self litters your mind with all the clutter you hold on to; all your past hurts and disappointments that build fear for the future. As the clutter chatters away, your body goes off on its own, engaging in tasks you don't even recognize it is doing. For your body and your mind can operate simultaneously in different directions.

Meet Kelly. Kelly stood up at a coffeehouse to read a passage from a book Kelly had written. Reaching the podium, Kelly felt a nervousness through the body. Kelly's mind forced one foot in front of the other and propelled the body forward. Kelly read and made it through two paragraphs before Kelly's Lower Self chimed in. Kelly could hear it; "No one is listening", and "No one is interested in what I am saying". Meanwhile, Kelly's eyes were looking at the page and Kelly's mouth was verbally communicating the words. It was the strangest sensation to play observer, aware of the body doing one thing and the mind doing another, while Kelly's Lower Self chattered on, reciting all the negative self-deprecation it had stored in its programming. Upon realizing what was happening, Kelly told the Lower Self it had no power here and asked the Higher Self to take over. Suddenly Kelly experienced the sensation of sliding back into the body's reality, fully conscious of reading to an audience. Kelly's reading was only seven minutes long, but in those seven minutes, Kelly mustered the courage to be true to the Higher Self, had a full-on battle with the Lower Self, wrestled with a childhood promise, told it to buzz off and came into balance with the body. Kelly left the podium seven minutes later, a different person.

When you live from the bigger perspective of the Higher Self, you see the world differently and interact with it in a whole new way. Getting there will not always be easy, though. You will face some very difficult truths about yourself along the way. You will be confronted by challenging moments when you must choose to honor your Higher Self or remain in your Lower Self. When you allow your Higher Self to steer you, it is quite possible, even probable, that others will feel threatened. Those who are not willing to change will view the new you as a personal attack on all they have settled for. Be prepared. Some will disappear from your life. Others will confront you or discount your journey, attempting to sabotage your commitment. Let these people go from your life. For you no longer require their presence to help keep you stuck. If you allow them to stay on, not only will they drag you back into your Lower Self, but they will occupy valuable space in your life that could go to someone who recognizes and honors the person you are becoming. Have faith. Operating in your truth will be a beacon for those who can recognize it, and new people will offer positive and supportive dynamics.

There will be some down time along your journey to your Higher Self. After the negative or fear-based individuals have given up on you and left your life, and before the positive, supportive ones migrate to you. Don't despair. Take the time to get to know all you are capable of, explore every possibility and trust in your Higher Self. Consciously remind yourself to view each moment from that higher perspective and tell the Lower Self to be quiet. It won't happen overnight, but by reminding yourself to view things only from your Highest Self, your perspective will change. You may find the hackles of your Lower Self still rise occasionally, but it is no longer occupying your thoughts, time and energy. If they rise, simply take a giant step back. Literally move your body backward. This will remind you to see the big picture and view the message only. In that way, you can retrain your brain to embrace the lesson, rather than the words, body language or behaviors of another person. It takes practice, so be patient. Like adjusting the lens on a camera, allow yourself time to adjust your lens to that of your Higher Self.

Exercise

In your journal, turn to a blank page and make a list of five ways you would like to be treated by others. Under each, in point form, write what another person would have to do for you to feel you are treated the way you want to be treated. Be specific. For example, if you write, "I want to be loved and valued". Write underneath exactly what another person would have to do or say for you to feel loved or valued by them.

Next, examine the specific actions or statements you wrote. Your assignment is to do everything on that list for yourself. If taking you out for a fancy dinner at an elegant restaurant is on your list, get yourself gussied up and take yourself out to that fancy restaurant. If having time alone is on your list, then give yourself a day off. Shut off the phone, turn off the television and stereo, and just be alone...see where it leads you.

Exercise

For the next three days, write what you notice in a journal or pocket-sized notepad. Don't think about it, just go about your business and when something briefly snatches your attention away from what you are doing, jot it down. It could be a picture or saying on a billboard, song lyrics stuck in your head, or an animal that crosses your path. It could be a random butterfly in your home or the bright pink rain boots of a child on the street. Start noticing what you notice.

On the fourth day, start another three-day cycle of documenting what you notice. But this time, write what you notice about yourself, whether you are teary-eyed watching a movie, getting inspiration from a conversation in a check-out line, or feel a sudden boost after receiving a compliment. Maybe your hackles rise as you get triggered by a comment from a co-worker, or you smile when you see an older couple holding hands. Perhaps you feel the weight lift when you see the sunset. Find joy by crawling into fresh, clean bedsheets after a long, hot shower. Document it all. Notice what brings you joy and what triggers your resistance. This exercise allows you to distinguish between the two lenses of the Lower and Higher Self and that puts you on the path to transformation.

Your Higher Self vibrates at the high frequency of feeling good. Your Lower Self vibrates at the low frequency of burden and gets triggered by anything that challenges its programmed way of being. Through this exercise, you learn what feels good for you and thus begin separating the two versions of you. You discover that what you notice is not as random as you may think. Your Higher Self sees what your Lower Self cannot. Suddenly song lyrics that play over and over in your mind present a solution to a problem you've been pondering. A billboard reveals an answer you have been looking for. A storefront decor offers the prescription for creativity.

In essence, you learn to consider everything that grabs your attention as a teacher, a voice from the highest version of you, a guide leading you to a better life. Things happen for a reason and that reason is to teach you to live in the highest version of your Highest Self. What you notice is the Higher Self bringing inspiration to your life. So, when something causes you to pause, even briefly, it is your Higher Self inviting you to explore the possibilities and open your perspective. All that is required of you is to notice and trust it.

7

GROWING INTO MORE.
THE SHIFT FROM IMAGE
TO IDENTITY

"Learning to trust SELF is about questioning the
integrity of who you believe yourself to be."
-Sky Stevens

Finally, you have come to realize that what had been labeled 'wrong' about you long ago is truly right. After a childhood of bending and twisting yourself to be more of what was important about you, you can finally distinguish the true from the false.

What was important about you framed the conditioning of your Synthetic Self. Such was seldom, if ever, important *to* you. Compromising and undermining that which is important *to* you was and still is, a grave disservice. The more you withhold what is important to you, the more significance you place on what others deem important about you. Over time, becoming dependent on another's perception to sustain your Synthetic Self's social existence.

That social existence defined your image as your Synthetic Self eclipsed your identity, creating a visual representation of what they expected you to be in order to gain inclusion, comfort, and care. It was their mental picture of you. Your Synthetic Self worked hard to interpret and create what others wanted to see. The adjustments came slowly. Shaped over time. And your learned self-image is the masterpiece of that. It feels a pat on the back when others notice something important about you and it adjusts to offer more of the same. When it concludes that nothing about you catches the attention of others, it throws itself mercilessly into self-doubt, unworthiness, shame, insignificance, uncertainty, and paralyzing indecision. Your image depends solely on instant gratification from others. It does not generate its own experiences or emotions. It does not function independently, only in a society-approved existence of job, home and family, where many opinions about you come from many directions, and it is in its glory adjusting to accommodate all of them.

The Natural Self, however, is where your identity rests. It has been with you all along, yet only seems to rise to the surface on those rare occasions when you are alone. The more time you spend alone, the more frequently you will glimpse your Natural Self's identity and the easier it will be to know. Being alone is a gift. It is an opportunity to build a relationship with the highest version of you. It is important to be alone, to have entire chapters of life in which you are free to unleash your authentic nature. Unfortunately, there is a Collective belief that being alone in a society where the Noah's Arc Syndrome runs rampant, means there is something wrong with you. The Noah's Arc Syndrome is the Collective belief characterized by a perpetual need for dependence and an inflicted fear of isolation. Those touched by this syndrome diminish solo travelers as unattractive, strange, and undesirable. Like a three-legged race, those inflicted require another to lean on, to leash to, to move forward with and be supported by. To co-create a unity that reduces two individuals into one. Yet some journeys you must do alone. Those who take such journeys count only on themselves. They stand on their own two feet with no need to lean. For they have witnessed what Noah's Arc Syndrome sufferers will never have the courage to see. Their truth.

Growing into more is a solitary activity. It stems from being curious about yourself, your true potential and capabilities, aka your true identity. Your distinguishing character. What makes you, you. Growing into more is about uncovering your strengths, gifts, intent, thoughts, and being conscious and deliberate in these. Growing into the Natural Self allows you to think, speak and act deliberately. It is self identity mastery. Growing into more requires the courage to unveil and embrace your truth. It is not for the faint of heart. No longer handing over your power (the responsibility for your image) but stepping into it. You cannot sit with another in a collective image and stand in your identity at the same time.

Imagine the freedom of being the center of your world where the only opinion of yourself that truly matters is your own. Where you call the shots in your own life. Where you alone dictate your happiness. Where what is important to you takes precedence over another's opinion of you. Where every action and word stems from the love centered in the identity of your Natural Self rather than from the fear of your Synthetic Self's constant struggle to measure up.

There is only love or fear. These are the only motivations to do anything. Your Natural Self's identity is driven by love. Not the romantic love you learned to seek through Collective beliefs, but a genuine love, a marveling appreciation of and a tenderness and warmth for you, by you. Most are not used to perceiving themselves through the eyes of love. They are used to celebrating a surface love that comes through Valentine's and anniversaries. For this Collective belief defines one's image through intimacy, romance and relationships. Yet the genuine, unconditional love of your Natural Self's identity is an appreciation of true beauty. Like the overwhelming beauty in the silence of a sunset. The complete admiration of a giant oak. The utter fascination with the perfection of a flower. Flowers grow side by side and bloom when it is time to bloom. They do not compete. They stand in their own beauty, doing what comes naturally, fulfilling their individual mission and living their inimitable life. This is the genuine love that exists within your Natural Self's identity, and it welcomes you to know yourself on this level.

To fully appreciate the distinction between identity (love) and image (fear) you need only to adjust what you see and how you view it. Let's use the image of Godzilla, to make this point. Everyone knows Godzilla, the menacing creature that stormed cities and swatted airplanes. Imagine you are standing alone at the end of a long hallway. At the other end is Godzilla, growling and roaring, while marching down the hall in your direction. Do you have the image in your mind? How does the fact that Godzilla is one-inch tall shift your image and how you perceive yourself in the situation? At such a sight, you might walk right up to it just to make sure it is real, but you would not experience fear. Your identity would laugh, viewing such a tiny roaring, growling creature to be cute. You may even try to pick it up.

Now, imagine Godzilla growling and roaring, marching down the hall in your direction. This time Godzilla is a foot tall. Would you respond differently to the one-foot Godzilla versus the one-inch Godzilla? Would you turn and run away screaming? Perhaps you might try to catch the creature in a box or a cage of some sort. Would fear come into play?

Imagine, now, a three-foot-tall Godzilla growling and roaring, marching down the hall in your direction. The difference between love and fear is the difference between acting and reacting. How tall would Godzilla have to be for you to perceive a threat? One inch? A foot? Three feet? Six feet? Ten feet? At what height do you shift from feeling confident in handling the situation (identity) to running away screaming (image)? At what point do you shift from "I got this" to "Wholly crap, this thing is going to eat me"? The difference between acting with love and reacting with fear is perception.

A perceived threat is a product of the Synthetic Self, your learned self-image. You learned early in life what to perceive as a threat and what to perceive as tenderness and warmth. To a child, any sudden movement or noise leaves an instant impression. If a burglar broke in wearing a Winnie-the-pooh mask and surprised a three-year-old, that child would grow up with a fear of Winnie-the-pooh. They would perceive it as a threat, scary or dangerous and incorporate this fear into their Synthetic Self's image. They would avoid Winnie at all costs and later even prevent their child from engaging in storybooks, decorations, stuffed animals or lunch pails that portray the Winnie image despite there being no real logic or reasoning behind the fear. This is where your conditioning, limited logic, observations, and experience help to mold the Synthetic Self. Not only were you exposed to the unspoken beliefs and fears of those who raised you, but you created promises, beliefs and fears based on your perceptions as well. It doesn't take much for the child-self to lock in an image perpetuated by its perception of another's body language, facial expression, volume or tone of voice. If you perceive something as a threat, even as an adult, no one can talk you out of it.

Real threats and perceived threats are different. A real threat is something that has the potential to cause harm. Real threats are such because they present a real possibility of physical injury, perhaps even death. Most humans react similarly to real threats. The body sweats, and there is shortness of breath or trembling. They might throw up or lose consciousness. The adrenals know a real threat when it comes.

Perceived threats, however, are in the eye of the beholder, just like beauty. These threats, aka fear, exist only within the image created through the conditioning, experience, and perception of the Synthetic Self. No one else can feel, sense, or notice the fear perceived by another. Your image may scream and jump on a stool at the sight of a spider, while another's identity may pick it up and carry it outside. Perceived threats stem from a childhood fear of harm. Fear is a complicated beast. Acknowledging it and exposing your fear-based image is an incredibly difficult thing to do. Most defend and justify when fear rises from within, even when no physical threat is present. When you get defensive, you must remind yourself that fear is just a perception of your Synthetic Self's fear-based image and use the WHY? exercise at the back of this chapter to shift into your Natural Self's identity.

The Synthetic Self's fear puts you at the mercy of life and condemns you to an image with no voice. Everywhere you look, there are crimes against you. Most are not real. The Synthetic Self installs them to keep you locked within its program. Remember, like attracts like. If your old promise is still alive and kicking, you will perceive only your Synthetic Self's need to keep the promise alive. You may justify, but believing the Synthetic Self's justifications is fatal to acknowledging your fear. Feeling wronged is justification in its finest light. Justifications redirect you, not anyone else. Stomping fear with a solid justification serves the Synthetic Self well. It will justify you right into an environment you don't even want.

As was touched on earlier, the most obvious identifier of a learned self-image is the use of 'I don't want' statements. *"I would go but I don't want to be the only one."* or *"I would say something, but I don't want to look bad."*. Such is a search for validation, absolving you of responsibility, choice, and control. These are self-inflicted reminders of your image based on a promise to be undeserving. It is self-deception. You may even put so much energy into stating what you don't want that all your energy goes into creating it. Meanwhile, there is no energy left over to manifest what you truly do want. Your focus becomes your reality. You may spend years wondering why things have happened to you, without ever realizing you are living through an image that attracts such a life or realizing that you have the power to change it.

To uncover your identity and put your image to rest, you must visit the past but not stay there. You must use your past as a teacher. Accept that nothing can be undone. View your previous responses, emotions, words and actions as the stepping stones that led you to this moment. How you use the past determines your present. You can embrace it as valuable learning, or you can try to move forward with one foot stuck in the unjust and unresolved muck from long ago. The choice is yours and you can make it now.

If you are ready to be all you truly are, and fully embrace your identity, you must consciously select the people, the environments and applications that support you being all that you innately are. You must be ferociously and compassionately honest with yourself and be diligent in your choices and actions, ensuring they are consistent with the highest version of your highest SELF. When you get off track, you can locate the threads that connect you to your authentic nature and gently bring yourself back to it. Let the identity of your essential nature guide your words, thoughts, feelings and actions, always. True power is not about winning, outsmarting, controlling, manipulating, or blaming other people or situations. True power is soft and quiet. It raises you to a higher level. True power is about being fully present, every moment of every day.

Standing in your power presents a reality that encompasses so much more than you're used to. So much more than the status quo allows. It puts every ability and capability at your fingertips. All the knowing and wisdom and gifts and lessons. Identity is the ultimate version of SELF. The Natural Self is positive and expansive. It is a lightness of being. Your identity is the innate knowing of your truth. It heeds your instincts. You problem-solve, invent, and create at will. You accept your gifts and freely share them with the world without a need for reciprocation, recognition, or payment. Identity honors

SELF as one with all life and, above all, trusts that its presence is purposeful and necessary.

Your identity knows no fear. It is trust personified. It responds to each moment as an opportunity to stand in the highest version of SELF, learning the lessons left to learn and sharing its gifts. It is both teacher and student combined. This innate version of SELF exists in both the visible (the physical form) and invisible (knowing, reasoning, intellect). Your identity is inclusive and complete. It is perfect. It allows nature to take its course. It is the part of you that knows there is a reason for everything, and that reason is to live in the highest version of SELF and to honor it.

Growing into more means finding the joy in living through identity. For it is the home to the high frequency emotions of serenity, confidence, worthiness, and gratitude. When your image is always seeking, there is little room for gratitude. But the attitude of gratitude is the foundation of your identity. It reverts things back to their basic form and finds the joy within. It is accepting, tolerant, understanding, and empathetic. It sees the bigger picture with a knowing that all is as it ought to be and trusts that everything that happens is for your highest good. It requires nothing from others to extend itself out with kindness.

Your identity is multifaceted. It is the part of you that lives spherically, in many directions at once. The part of you that accepts its presence as an integral part of Nature, and knows its value is constant and independent of others. While the value of your Synthetic Self's image increases and decreases based on someone else's ability to see it. Your image is the head-dweller version of you, your Lower Self, and is never at peace.

Growing into more means moving along your identity's path with gratitude, humility, honor, and integrity. A path that recognizes and accepts each human has their journey and you must not interfere. Identity is the part of you that does not get dragged into the drama of another's Synthetic Self. It lives life through the passion of existence, through the pure joy of being, taking in all the colors, smells, sounds and occurrences along the way.

You have the means to live fully in your truth, minimizing the extent to which you engage in your conditioning. You are here for a purpose; to observe yourself and get to know who you truly are. No one can do the work for you. No one else can find the place where you feel most like yourself. No one can notice what you notice or recognize the signs that were meant just for you. No one else can fulfill your life's mission, extend your unique gift to the world, or learn the specific lessons you are here to learn. You are alone on this path.

No, it is not easy, yet it is not difficult either. All that is required is the desire for change, the desire to live differently than you currently do. You cannot view your life through the lens of your image, as a constant reflection of your need for validation, and view your life through the lens of your identity, as a mirror of the lessons you need to learn to live in the highest version of you, at the same time. You cannot live in fear (image) and truth (identity) at the same time. You can, however, switch to the lens of your Natural Self's identity whenever you want. Just because you made a promise and adopted a man-made image to show the world, doesn't mean your Natural Self's identity went anywhere. It has been within you the whole time. There is no personal growth or development required. All it takes is an uncovering of your identity and a desire to know it better than anyone else. That is where your true power lies. When you know yourself on that level, you can never be hurt because you keep your power to wound. You can never be triggered because you accept every aspect of your identity. You can never be less-than ever again.

Exercise

In your journal write three things you are waiting for right now. Don't think about it, just jot them down. Then close your journal and put it down. There is no need to read what you wrote. Just let it be for the moment.

Now, imagine that every action and word stems from either the love in the Natural Self or the fear in the Synthetic Self. That's it. All or nothing. Black or white. Love or fear.

The fear in the Synthetic Self is complex, so let's start with love. For the next hour, play observer in your life. Notice which of your actions and words stem from an intense feeling of deep affection, fondness, tenderness and warmth. It may take a bit of practice, so be patient. Once you are aware of how and when you express genuine love, you can deliberately incorporate true interest and appreciation through loving actions and words into your daily life.

Unfortunately, those words and actions you could not label as love, are based in fear. Not an easy thing to admit, but critical to know. If you find you respond with fear more often than genuine love, you are not alone. Most of us do. But a conscious and deliberate intent can easily remedy that.

Go back to your journal and read the three things you are waiting for. Which of these are based in love and which are based in fear? For example, those created consciously out of love might include waiting for the meal to cook that you are making to nourish your body or waiting for your daughter to get home safely from her first date. While those created in fear may include waiting for another to be the first to call after an argument or waiting for someone to stop monopolizing your time. If you become defensive or start justifying during this process, write the defense or justification and apply the WHY? exercise below to uncover the fear.

WHY? Exercise

When something troubles your mind and you hear an incident or conversation replaying over and over in your head and your emotions are in full swing, write it all down. What you write while you are all charged up will be your first layer of defense; the auto-pilot response of your Synthetic Self. If you're like the rest of us, it will be a tangent of *he did,* and *she said* and *they should have.* This is a wonderful place to start. When you have exhausted your tirade, move your pen to a new line and write the word WHY?. Then answer the question. When you exhaust that answer, write the word WHY? underneath and again, write what comes to mind. By continuing this process, you will uncover the layers of your learned identity and reveal what you are truly wanting out of the situation or from the other person. Then you will be ready to re-visit the situation with your intent clear and your emotions calm. Do not judge what is written. Don't even read it! By reading what you have written, you will get dragged back into your own drama. Instead, think of it as the skin of an onion. Each time you write WHY? you are peeling off another layer of the Synthetic Self's programming. What matters is the final statement at the end of it all that reveals your identity. Your genuine feelings and intent. That is your truth. Celebrate this AH-HA moment when it arrives. Only then can you set your true intent for the direction of the highest version of you.

8

ALTERING INTENT

"Owning intent is like catching the wind.
It requires a conscious fabric to fully
absorb its direction and strength."
-Sky Stevens

Choice. That beautiful luxury so few recognize in their lives. From getting out of bed in the morning to what you have for dinner, you have choice. It takes focus to recognize the presence of choice and courage to accept the responsibility of it. Even you, uttered, at some point, the, *"I had no choice"* excuse, hoping to get yourself off the proverbial hook. Yet, when you defer a choice in such a way, you make a choice to defer. When you blame, you make the choice to blame. When you hand over your power, you make that choice too. Even the absence of choice is a choice to relinquish choice. Choice is inescapable. It exists every minute of every day, and you can learn to exercise it well.

It is the Covert belief that blocks the image from making good choices. Too often, the attachment to the outcome lodged in your Synthetic Self clouds any reasoning, and the familiar antics of its habitual thinking take over. Your identity, however, has full appreciation and acceptance of choice. Steered by the Natural Self, you have the power to step in, or step out, of every interaction that is or is not, for your highest good and the power to be conscious about it.

There is only a split second between stimulus and response, and in it lays the fabric of choice. In that split second, you choose to either let the Covert belief have its way or reclaim your power and step boldly into the Natural Self. Ultimately, the choice stems from intent. Taking ownership of that intent is the key to dispelling the patterns of the past. It requires a level of truth that takes you way beyond your comfort zone.

As a child, you were seldom, if ever, encouraged to acknowledge the intent behind your thoughts, words or actions because the intent was not influential to the posturing of the coping mechanisms buried within the habitual heritage of your early environment. With the familiar reactions accepted and encouraged, nobody questioned them. Your Synthetic Self blindly adopted the familiar reactions, phrases and postures as acceptable and incorporated these into your image. Now that you have identified and taken ownership of the Synthetic Self, you can take steps to stop its *auto-pilot* reactions. To do this, you must expand the moment between stimulus and response by consciously increasing the time between a trigger and an *auto-pilot* reaction. It is a skill learned through practice. This skill allows you to unveil your intent within a split second and make a conscious choice of what happens next. You must practice drawing out that moment to buy yourself time to be objective about your intent. Is your intent to reduce the Synthetic Self's power by *attending to* the Natural Self or to fuel it by permitting its control over your thoughts, words, and actions? The direction and strength of your intent sets the foundation for that choice. The first time you halt an *auto-pilot* reaction through a consciously created intent is the first time you choose to honor SELF. That is a really big deal!

Intent, in its purest form, is the motivation behind any word, action, or thought. It is the desire to act in pursuit of a specific goal. You must bring your intent out in the open and examine it carefully to determine exactly what you are feeling and wanting in each moment and whether it stems from image or identity. With practice, you can lengthen the moment between stimulus and response, pushing the pause button on all else and granting yourself time to make this decision. It is the ultimate opportunity to witness the Synthetic Self and reveal what it will do or say to keep the old patterns alive.

By observing your intent, being honest about what you truly want, and learning to express it, you can align who you are on the inside with what you show on the outside. You can pay attention to yourself and your words, feelings, and body. Your body will never betray you. It will always tell the truth about your identity. Note how your body responds to events and conversations. Keeping a journal helps. Not only will the practice of writing actively engage your body as the mind processes, but it's a great way to get to know your body. Notice if or when your hand pauses as you write, you are writing something false about yourself. Notice if your hand switches between printing and writing or if the penmanship alters, this may say something about what you are writing as well. Your hands will not betray your truth, so by writing feelings out, you take ownership of them and by taking ownership, you can push yourself to the edge of your character just to see if it is a sustainable place to live. The harder you push, the more you reveal about SELF. You are capable of things you haven't dared dream of, and never suspected. You are capable of so much more than your image believes yourself to be and know so much more than you allow yourself the luxury of knowing.

The Largo Notice Principle is a strategy for slowing down the moments between stimulus and response. Identifying the chatter of the Synthetic Self is necessary for understanding your intent. Listen to it, and recognize the programming, but do not react to it. This is the first step in applying the Largo Notice Principle to your daily life. The main consideration of this principle is that the Synthetic Self does not warrant judgment or bias. Instead, you must embrace it with compassion, love and gratitude, recognizing it as a creation of your child-self. So concentrate on recognizing the unique voice of your learned image.

This inadvertently pauses the moment between the Synthetic Self and its typical pattern of response. Within that pause, you focus on forming a question of how to honor your highest SELF and listen for the answer before you speak or act. The Largo Notice Principle slows the stimulus/response movement down to a slow and dignified tempo, allowing you to consider your child-self's fear lodged in your Synthetic Self's image, and consider the highest version of SELF, your feelings and body in the moment, and consciously choose which to listen to and follow. *Pause and perceive before deed* is the mantra of the Largo Notice Principle.

To break the ties that keep your image in place and your promise alive, you must first witness and acknowledge your child-self's perception, the emotion that it experienced and the string that continues to tie them together. Perception and emotion occurring simultaneously are what complete the agenda of your promise, thus locking the perception and emotion together as your image. Like mittens tied together with a string, perceptions and emotions are bound to each other. Anything and everything that jogs the perception from long ago automatically triggers the original emotional response, and vice versa.

These are incredibly difficult to separate but with the *pause and perceive before deed* process of the Largo Notice Principle, it can be done. Of course, the initial conditioning and the *auto-pilot* life you have learned is certainly easier, for you already know how to live there. You are familiar with and know how to function in, dishonoring environments and can slip silently into them without batting an eye. Dishonoring SELF goes with the familiar territory of your learned self-image and began the minute you made your initial promise. By using the *pause and perceive before deed* practice, the Natural Self steps in to guide you through the process of change.

You require guidance to reveal what lies at the core of your learned self-image. That guidance comes through various teachers and circumstances until you are ready to see what needs to be seen. The biggest obstacle, of course, is that the Synthetic Self believes its thinking and perceptions are always right. You have been living in your Synthetic Self for so long; you see only through that lens and perceive what you see as a true representation of yourself. To counteract your image, you must learn to question everything you think and know to be true.

You treat the world the way you treat yourself, so you must dig deep. You must check in with your Natural Self's identity to know how to act, and what to say, to ensure you are sending the highest version of SELF out into the world. After all, what you put out into the world is what you will be on the receiving end of. Ensure the language on the tip of your tongue accurately describes and reflects your highest SELF. Language is often used to decorate the Synthetic Self's image, making you appear more or sometimes less than you are, which means you must pay close attention. To exaggerate or understate an experience is to admit you do not regard your experience as legit or worthy, which is the ultimate betrayal of the Natural Self.

There is no better way to honor SELF than to have the courage to present yourself truthfully and authentically by considering the precision of your language. You must mean what you say and say what you mean.

Your Synthetic Self will fight it, guaranteed. It will lure you back into its programming every chance it gets. But you can reclaim your footing with the use of discernment. Without discernment, you remain wedged at the mercy of your Synthetic Self, yet secretly craving a different experience. True discernment allows you to take a step back and observe. Through discernment, the Natural Self can review the subtleties and make a well-informed decision. In short, discernment offers your identity the power to see what is not available to your Synthetic Self's image. It gives you the choice to spend time and energy replaying and re-feeling the emotional rollercoaster of the past, or consciously investing the time and energy into stepping into your Natural Self's identity.

When pulled by a destructive influence, in the present or from the past, a helpful practice is to take one giant step back. To literally pick up your foot and step back. This simple tool puts space between you and the destructive influence that demands your attention. This mantra is also helpful. "Everything that happens is for my highest good." Through rhythm, repetition and practice, you can drill this intent in, switching your lens from image to identity. You can wake up every morning, smile, and say out loud, "Everything that happens is for my highest good" then go about your day, open and ready for your brilliance to radiate out to the world. Repeating it over and over applies this new intent to every aspect of your life. You will witness changes instantly.

This phrase alone will not transform you. Shifting your intent is only half of the equation. You must also shift the way you treat yourself. By treating SELF with the kindness it deserves, your actions will match the new intent. Typically, one of your Collective beliefs defines kindness as performing a deed with no need for praise or recognition. True kindness is not so glamorous. It is not nice or munificent. It is not one random act to be executed when or how you choose with the sole purpose of putting a smile on the face of another. True kindness does not sit like this, on the shelf of ego, bypassing acclaim just this once, for just this one act. Kindness is a lifestyle choice that does not involve doing. It involves being.

True kindness comes from within. It is a practice of being generous with SELF. And it begins by trusting in a part of yourself that you cannot see, smell, taste, or touch. It is to stop caring what others think or do, and instead, focus your *attending to* completely on being the best version of you. It is to treat yourself better than you treat anyone else. It is to grant yourself permission to exist in your natural form. To be independent of conditioning, the promise and the Synthetic Self. It involves the proper consideration of every thought, every emotion, every word and every action to ensure each stem from the Natural Self. It is a knowing, a trust in SELF, regardless of what the Synthetic Self says. It is the adoption of an observer's role within your life to ensure every aspect of your being is authentic.

Kindness toward SELF is the difference between time passing and a life truly lived! It is not being nice, generous or thoughtful. A play of weakness or hardship cannot extract it from another person. Treating SELF with kindness results from the realization that you are deserving of all that is good. This inspires a greater kindness towards SELF, which inspires a deeper relationship with SELF, and a new realization that SELF is deserving of even greater consideration, which inspires an even greater kindness towards SELF, and so on, increasing the energy and vibration you extend out to the world, thus attracting a higher energy and vibration back. The Natural Self expands in this way until the Synthetic Self is no longer visible. This is the key to liberating yourself from the weight of habitual heritage.

SELF kindness is a lifetime commitment. It is a way of being. A way of living that employs the entirety of a person. It requires a wakeful will and a determined practice. Kindness requires adeptness in viewing the bigger picture. Those who claim kindness, or trumpet their endeavors, do so through the Synthetic Self's image. SELF kindness does not broadcast. It radiates from within. It is an expansive way of living achieved through an honest rendering of SELF. To simply crave a richer and fuller life is not enough. You must evoke the solicitude to vacate your current life and start anew. It means giving up all that you are for all that you may become. It demands a huge leap of faith to trust yourself entirely.

The conditioning of the Synthetic Self does not allow for such an undertaking. The more it considers change, the more familiar your current life appears. The more familiar your current life appears; the safer it seems. The safer it seems, the more secure you feel. This is the way of the Synthetic Self's image. It waits for other people to change. To suddenly see the error of their ways and finally acknowledge its value so it feels accepted, cared for and loved. It revels in the chaos of hostile environments and attracts destructive influences. It perceives life as a struggle. It continues in a downward spiral until it sabotages the dream of something greater to once again convince you to simply stay put. If you truly wish for the freedom of a different life, you must observe yourself and accept, without judgment, what you have created thus far. Did you renovate your home but not your way of being? Do you take care of your car but not your body? Have you refreshed your wardrobe but not your mindset? When you understand you can renovate, refresh and take care of SELF, amazing things happen. It is the perception of experience that determines the quality of your life.

You must take an inventory of your life. When you are living consciously and allowing life to unfold for your highest good, the perception of life expands, and you witness your magnificent nature. This is the Natural Self's way. It stimulates the senses and gathers information through them. As a result, you are fully present in every second, recording far more experiences in the memory than the Synthetic Self would even know was possible.

The Natural Self explores the biggest picture of your identity, resulting in a richer, fuller experience. It infuses each experience with honorable intent. The Synthetic Self sees only what its conditioning sees. It views each experience as a separate element in your life. The simple truth is you cannot have both roots and wings. The wings of the Natural Self allow you to soar to the heights of your full potential. The roots of the Synthetic Self keep you stuck in place. What the Natural Self sees is seldom what the Synthetic Self perceives. The difference between roots and wings is knowing the motivation behind each word, thought, and action and determining the source of your intent. Do not hand over your power by giving someone else the responsibility for how you feel about yourself.

You have the power to change your perspective and show up in a way that makes you feel good about yourself. You have the choice and power to be the person you want to be. Remember, you must take responsibility for your actions, reactions, and words. Take responsibility for yours and let others take responsibility for theirs. It is not your job to keep everyone happy; it is your job to keep you happy, to follow the path of your Natural Self. Check in with yourself and clarify your intent. Intent is the key. Before you react to someone's hurtful words, check your intent. Admit what your reaction is, but don't execute it. Instead, analyze your intent. Be honest with yourself. Have you selected your words to hurt that person as they have hurt you? If so, before you open your mouth, remember that you have a choice. You can choose to be the bigger person. You can choose to receive that person with love and warmth, or lower yourself to their level, taking on the insecurities reflected in their words. How another shows up has nothing to do with you.

Exercise

Paying attention to the senses is a great way to extend kindness to yourself. It not only adds a new level of engagement, but it slows life down and allows you to be fully present in each moment. It connects you to your body, offering a much-needed rest from the head-dweller thinking of the Synthetic Self. For one week, treat yourself with kindness by turning everyday moments into phenomenal experiences. Listen to the birds. Smell the fragrance of shampoo. Savor the taste of food. Experience the fabric of clothing. You do not have to fly to some exotic place to rock your world with a new experience. Through SELF kindness, everyday tasks become full experiences, and you learn to appreciate your life in a whole new way. By consciously observing your taste, touch, smell, sight and sound, you are on your way to living in the highest version of your highest SELF.

Exercise

All things are made of energy, including the human body. Here we explore your relationship to different forms of energy to determine the truth behind your relationship to SELF.

Open your journal and draw a line down the middle of the page. On the left side of the page, write what comes to mind when you hear the word 'food'. Food is a form of energy. The word 'food' may define nourishment, grocery shopping, preparing, cooking, nutrition, eating, diet, and all aspects of food. Really think about how you define 'food'. When you hear the word, do you sigh or salivate? Is food a burden or an adventure? Without judgment about what, how or when you eat, simply consider your relationship with food.

For example, do you regard the nutrients of food, eating only to supply your body with the fuel it requires to run efficiently? Do you consider food a friend, a comfort, eating when you are stressed, lonely or anxious? Perhaps you deny yourself nourishment when you feel guilty, nervous, or worried. Maybe food is social, a venue to meet with friends. Or maybe food is synonymous with prominence, and you contribute to your social image by frequenting luxurious restaurants, ordering specialties of the palate, and proclaiming a superior knowledge of fine wines. Maybe you find food an inconvenience that interrupts action. A necessary evil, causing you to consume power bars, processed food products or food supplements to trick your body into believing it is satisfied. Do you eat three square meals a day, swearing by a regimented food guide or diet? Do you graze all day long? Do you prepare and enjoy the food you eat? Do you devour whatever is quick and easy? Do you eat takeout often? Visit fast-food joints? Do you prepare a lunch or buy your lunch each day? Every aspect of your relationship with food is worth exploring, so take the time to really examine it.

Once the left column is complete, on the right-hand side of the page, write the relationship you would like to have with food. When that is complete, move to the lower right side of the page, and make a list of the reasons you do not currently have the relationship with food you would like to have. Remember there is no judgment here, so be honest.

Let's move on to another form of energy- time. Just as you did with 'food', explore your relationship with 'time'. Turn to a blank page and draw a line down the middle of it. On the left side of the page, write what comes to mind when you hear the word 'time'. Do you embrace every moment? Do you hustle through each day? Do you set aside time for important things? Do you pack the important things into an already hectic day? Do you justify procrastination with phrases like '*I should take time to...*'? Maybe you use time as your playground scapegoat with phrases like '*if I can find the time*'? Do you define time by a to-do list or tasks? Have a day planner or phone attached to you always? Do you schedule your life? Or sit back and go with the flow? Do you rush around at the last minute or arrive with time to spare? Are you notoriously late or consistently early? Consider how you treat time or perhaps how time treats you. A note, be honest. No one with a cell phone in their hand 24-7 truly goes with the flow! Do you have time, want time, spend time, need time, make time, waste time, or manage time like a wild colt, reining it in to cater to your thoughts, ego or bank account?

Once that is complete, on the top of the right-hand side of the page, write the relationship you would like to have with time. When that is complete, move to the lower right side of the page, and make a list of the reasons you do not currently have the relationship with time you just wrote above. Why or why don't you respond to time like you want to?

What about health? Turn to a blank page and draw a line down the middle of the page. On the left side of the page, write what comes to mind when you hear the word 'health'. What is the first thing that comes to mind, and why? Are you experiencing ailments or conditions that could be emotion-based? Take a close look at what ails you. Could there be an emotional component that, until now, has been overlooked? For example, when the muscles cramp, is it a reaction to an inflexible mindset or a lack of hydration? Health is a marriage between the emotional and the physical; a combination of what you eat and what's eating you. To truly improve your physical and emotional health, it is important to distinguish the difference.

To determine whether an ailment is emotional or physical in nature, you may use a blank page and divide the page into three columns. In one column, write any tension or discomfort that your body is experiencing this minute. In the next column, write what you have eaten today, including time and amounts. In the final column, jot down a list of worries, anxieties, joys, or excitements that you are experiencing today. Go back over all three columns and note how each corresponds to the other. By doing this exercise daily, you will gain a better understanding of your health, how you define it and what it truly means to you.

Returning to your 'health' page, on the top right-hand side of the page, write the relationship you would like to have with your health. When that is complete, move to the lower right side of the page, and make a list of the reasons you do not currently have the level of health you just wrote above. What prevents you from having the state of health written above?

Let's move on to another form of energy and explore 'creativity'. Turn to a blank page. At the top of the page, answer this question, do you consider yourself a creative person? A yes or no answer will do. Then draw a line down the middle of the page. On the left side of the page, write what comes to mind when you hear the word 'creativity'. Do you use your imagination or original ideas to produce something that others can see, feel, taste, or touch? Do you paint, write, invent, design, fix or work with wood? Is creativity a stress reliever or a source of stress? What do you do with what you produce? Do you sell it, store it, hide it, display it, or give it away? Do you hang it on the walls or cover it with a tarp in the garage? It is important to gain as much insight into your creativity as possible, so be specific. Write as much as you can about the role creativity plays in your life, how you express it or repress it, and the emotional outlet it offers or the emotion it creates.

While you're at it, jot down whether you engage in other activities while those creative juices are flowing. Is the TV or radio on at the same time? Do you talk on the phone while allowing your imagination to speak? Perhaps you set aside a structured time for creativity and deny yourself nourishment until the time is over. Perhaps you eat first and push creativity aside until later and then get sidetracked before getting there. Whatever your typical creative practices are, it is important to be honest about them.

Now, on the top right-hand side of the page, write the relationship you would like to have with creativity. Do you dream of learning or returning to some creative practice? Is there something creative you have always wanted to try? When that is complete, move to the lower right side of the page, and make a list of the reasons you do not currently have the relationship with creativity you just wrote above.

Let's try another. Your relationship with Nature is perhaps the most defining of all. How you treat Nature is ultimately how you treat yourself. Turn to a new page and draw a line down the middle of the page. On the left side of the page, write what comes to mind when you hear the word 'Nature'. What is your relationship with Nature? Do you have a living room full of plants? Do have a backyard full of bird feeders? Do you marvel when a fly lands on you? Or do you plaster your space with fly tape and bug zappers? Do you hide from the sun or soak it up? Do you use rodent killers or humane traps? If you hunt, do you hunt for food or a trophy? Do you spend your time outdoors or inside? Your relationship with Nature speaks volumes about the programming of your Synthetic Self. For how you treat one life form is how you treat all life forms, including your own.

Once that is complete, on the top right-hand side of the page, write the relationship you would like to have with nature. Do you have copies of National Geographic stashed away, secretly hoping to visit wild places one day? When that is complete, move to the lower right side of the page, and make a list of the reasons you do not currently have the relationship with Nature you just wrote above.

Your relationship to Nature represents your relationship to your Synthetic Self or your Natural Self depending on which you presently dwell in. Those who choose to disrespect and devalue themselves seldom nurture pets, houseplants or beautiful gardens, while those who embrace their own life are more likely to take in strays, foster beautiful yards and spend time in the outdoors. Just pay attention and you will see it.

It is time to do a quick review of what you have written about your relationships with food, time, health, creativity and Nature. Flip back through the pages of your journal and review what you wrote for each aspect of your life. Is there a common theme that runs through the lists? For example, when you feel rushed or pressured by time, do you deny yourself nourishment from either food or creativity? When your emotional or physical health has your attention, do you feel creative or go outside to revel in nature? When you are engrossed in creativity, do you forget to eat or lose track of time? By recognizing common themes, you can gain a deeper understanding of how you treat energy, so take some time and look for common themes amongst the lists so far.

Now it is time to explore the relationship you have with money. On a blank page of your journal, write any physical or emotional responses you have to the word 'money'. There are no right or wrong answers here. List as many aspects of your relationship with money as you can and leave room for others you may think of later. Does time seem to move faster when finances are low or speed up? Do you resent money and the need for it? What do you do if you have more money than you expected? Is it the same thing you would do with more food, better health or greater creativity? In what way does money impact your life? Is it a necessary evil? Is it your ticket to freedom? Do you enjoy money and all it stands for? Do you resent money and having to work for it? What do you use the money for?

There are no judgments about what, how or when you save or spend. Here, you are simply considering your relationship with money. Start with the basics. Do you receive a regular pay cheque? Do you work contract work, receiving money only when a job comes along? Do you live within a budget? Do you enjoy money while you have it and then go back to work when the money pot runs dry? Take some time to write a list of where and how you make money.

Add two more columns and use one to list what you do with money once you have it. For example, do you love money as a friend, enjoying its company and comfort? Do you save it? Do you spend it? Do you spend beyond your bank balance, living a life of easy monthly payments? Do you hoard money, stashing your cold hard cash under your mattress or in a container in your freezer where it won't burn in a fire? When money is abundant, do you engage with others more frequently, join in community events and enjoy healthy foods? When the balance is more than you expected, does life become light? Do you find yourself giddy or euphoric? Do you revel in the joy of living? Do you suddenly feel tall, slim and in great shape? Does your self-esteem increase when money is abundant?

In the other column, explore how you feel and act when money is scarce. Does your life seem limited when money is scarce? Does your refrigerator stay empty for days as you justify using up the canned goods? Do you spend anyway, buying on credit or borrowing money from others? If your bank account dwindles, does your self-esteem plummet? Does your once attractive and healthy form suddenly seem overweight, short, and out of shape, allowing shame to reach for the ice cream to drown your sorrows? Does your career seem challenging when finances are? Do you panic and retreat from opportunities to socialize and engage with others?

Once you have made your money list, compare it to your lists about food, time, health, creativity and Nature. You may find similarities between the lists. For example, you may find your relationship with creativity is like your relationship with time and money; you never seem to have enough. You may find your relationship with money is like your relationship with food; hoarding food as you hoard money or denying yourself nourishment as you deny yourself luxury. Try to be objective when you read through your lists.

Sit with it. Embrace it. Own it. This is your current relationship with money, food, time, health, creativity and Nature. To build a healthy and nurturing relationship with yourself, it is critical to understand and accept your current relationship with energy. Only then can it be changed by altering your intent to embrace your Natural Self.

9

LEARNING TO TRUST
THE NATURAL SELF

"We must learn to trust our instinctual nature as our one true source."
-Sky Stevens

What you have learned so far is incredible. You have defined your Synthetic Self, dismantled its armor, uncovered your Natural Self, adopted its identity and taken great strides to live through honoring your intent and treating yourself with kindness. There is just one more piece left to the equation and that is trust.

Trusting the Natural Self, your authentic SELF is about learning to be, not do. It's about taking all the energy you put into *doing* and put it towards *being* who you uniquely are. Trusting what is important *to* you, not what is important *about* you. You must learn to marvel at being the person you innately are and to trust that person above all others. Your truth will, in fact, set you free. Free to think, speak, and act deliberately. Free to stand back and observe all that life offers. Free to find humor in your humanness. Your mind will relax, and your body will come into balance. Trust your inner knowing. It is your one true source.

Where you place your trust dictates the life that follows. Will you continue to trust that what you learned about you is all that you are and all that you will ever be? Will you continue to trust that being less-than is the most you deserve? Do you still trust another's opinion over your own? Or are you ready to trust your truth and embrace the life that follows? Are you ready to leap with complete faith that your Higher Self will guide you and trust it completely? Dreaming of a richer and fuller life requires the consideration of such questions. Living a richer and fuller life requires you to have a level of faith and trust in yourself that is like nothing you have ever experienced before. Such a critical approach to deliberate living hones a proficiency in SELF that allows for the rendering of good. It feeds an unwavering conviction that allows for SELF kindness, regardless of the whimpering persistence of the Synthetic Self as it fades into the background.

In your truth and Natural Self you are confident, strong and powerful, walking with your head up and being proud of your authentic SELF. Things don't bother you like they used to. You let people say their silly comments and do bizarre things with their lives, knowing they are on their own path, and you are on yours. But occasionally, you will get triggered by something that crashes through your paradise. That old Synthetic Self will rear its ugly head, and you will come to a grinding halt. It's okay. It is just a test to see if you have learned the lessons that were put in front of you. Take a breath and watch the drama unfold. Be still. You now have the tools to observe your Synthetic Self at work. Since you don't live in it anymore, you can now watch from the sidelines. How glorious to have the roles reversed! To live in your Natural Self instead of glimpsing it and glimpsing your Synthetic Self instead of living in it.

It has been a long road to get here, but you did it. Fighting the fear of success was the most challenging. Appreciating that you have resilience and power within takes a bit of persuasion. It requires attention; a keen observation of how you treat yourself every moment of every day. Treating yourself with the kindness necessary to embrace your true gifts takes great determination. It demands a commitment to unleash your innate power and honor it. That level of SELF trust is like a hall pass from childhood conditioning. It liberates you from the burden of a learned self-image and views you through lighter eyes. The food tastes better; the air smells fresher; the colors are more vibrant, and you can, at last, breathe.

Trusting your Natural Self means trusting the innate knowing of SELF based on its truth. Recognizing it as an element of Nature, subject to the Earth's cycles, with inherent features, and qualities like instinct, wisdom and intuition. Trusting the Natural Self means trusting your capacity to explore the plane between the visible

Sky Stevens

(the physical form) and the invisible (knowing, reasoning, intellect). Trusting your Natural Self means trusting your perfection and not bothering with the opinions of others. You hold more potential than you realize. Trusting your Natural Self means moving along your path with grace, humility, honor, and integrity. It means being passionate about your existence and finding pure joy in simply being. Trusting your Natural Self means releasing the Synthetic Self's need to control and instead allowing nature to take its course, trusting that the course will lead to the highest version of your highest SELF. Trusting your Natural Self means finally giving SELF permission to be free, and that feels good!

Feeling good cannot be faked, fabricated, pretended, engineered, designed, or even contrived. It exists only in the senses and the body. The slowing of the heart rate, the release of the shoulders, the slow steady breath, the complete lapse of time. Feeling good comes in those fragile moments when you have complete faith in your Natural Self. The truth of the matter is that feeling good is a good feeling because you feel most like yourself and revel in the goodness of your innate truth. It is more than just telling the truth. It is living in it.

The moment you feel most like yourself, you know with certainty you are experiencing the Natural Self and trust is inevitable. Your focus shifts from the outside world to the best version of SELF. You innately know who you are within, and by honoring it, understand how it naturally brings out the highest good in everyone who crosses your path. Trusting the Natural Self means being able to assess situations, and then consciously choose to accept them as they are or refuse to take part in them. Trusting the Natural Self is about standing tall and being still, regardless of the surrounding chaos. It is about discovering what makes you feel most like yourself and bringing it to the forefront of your life.

To do this, start with a physical place that you feel most like yourself. This is the key. For you, it might be the ocean, a garden, a mountaintop, a forest or a meadow with wildflowers. It is the place where you lose sense of time and space. It is the place you visit and become one with until suddenly you snap back to reality and exclaim, "*Gee, what time is it?*" It is a place in which you are totally engaged with no thoughts about how much money is in the bank, what bills need paying, what is for dinner or what is on the to-do list. Find that place where you feel most like yourself. Once you recognize it, the rest is easy. Go there. Go there often. Notice your thoughts when you are there, your actions, and how you feel and memorize them. Lock it in and embrace the 'you' you find there. This is your identity. It is the gateway to living full-time in your Natural Self. It is the 'you' to trust implicitly, for it is your truth. When you harness that trust, you shine like never before. There will be a shift in the way you relate to others and the way they relate to you. That sensation of feeling most like yourself is now your baseline for everything else in your life.

It takes some practice, but once you can identify that

'you', you can incorporate it into your daily life. The more you feel most like your SELF, the more you live in your Natural Self. The more time you spend in your Natural Self, the less time you engage in the programming of your Synthetic Self. With frequency and repetition, feeling most like yourself can replace the Synthetic Self altogether as you adopt a new lens through which to view your life.

Any location that causes a tightness in your chest, a tense muscle in the back of your neck, or a soreness of your lower back, is not a location that benefits your identity. These physical reminders are not present in the peace and contentment of the place where you feel most like yourself. They are your body telling you that something is not right. Do you experience these reminders in your relationships? In your workplace? In your home? In your car? If you answered yes to any of these, it might be time to make some changes. Where your body creates reminders signifies the locations, situations, and people attracted through your Synthetic Self. Now that you live in your Natural Self, it is your beacon for attracting new locations, situations, and people who align with you being most like yourself, so let the others go.

One way to prolong the sensation of feeling most like yourself is to identify your superpower and harness it. Like a Marvel comic hero, your superpower began from an incident. It started as a coping mechanism honed to overcome a perpetual obstacle. For example, because of early experiences, self-preservation may have taught you to pay attention to details. If your early environment was unpredictable, you may have learned to watch for small signs that a storm was coming and prepare yourself ahead of time for the eruption. As you grew, the attention to detail grew into a practice of discernment, your superpower. As an adult, you can choose when and where to use your superpower of discernment.

What started as a remedy for negative emotion can now be a gift. You may be unwilling to accept the power learned through self-preservation as a true gift, allowing such a gift to wilt at the hand of your Synthetic Self. If this is the case, your childhood experience weighs in on your life. You cannot see or recognize a skill developed from early repetition as birthing some silver lining. If you live under the burden of perceived negative experiences; childhood abuse, relationships failed, jobs expired, quarrels past and dreams postponed, the weight on your shoulders and in your heart can be so heavy you can barely stand up straight.

By refusing ownership of a gift exposed and refined in early childhood, the resolve of your Synthetic Self reaches out to the world for support. You seek someone or something to prop yourself up against; a spouse, a job, a religion or community, anything that will sustain your Synthetic Self and its purpose. Temporarily upright, you rely on another's income, another's generosity, another's compassion, or another's acquisitions to sustain the familiar, the safety, the security of a way of life left unchanged. As time passes, the burden of reliance creates an additional weight on your over-burdened body. The guilt of compromise, the dishonor of settling and the shame of choosing easy over SELF, all add to an over-burdened psyche. Your human experience, stretched beyond its society-approved limitations, folds in on itself, further burdening the perceived hardship with alcohol, drugs, sugar and other addictive numbing agents to induce an illusion of joy. The perception of care, benevolence, sympathy and worth is the paycheck to such a compromised life, with the search for moral, physical, financial or emotional charity squandering true living. Without such a commitment to the alteration of lifestyle, your Natural Self lies on the verge of extinction, functioning on an emotional poverty line and buried under the infliction of childhood conditioning. You doubt, question, compromise and deny your SELF as you were taught to by the masters of your early years.

This picture can change dramatically when you incorporate trust into the equation. By embracing a skill learned through self-preservation, you can rise and view that skill as a superpower, trusting it completely and consciously using it for good and positive change in your life. It is important to identify the coping skill adopted by your child-self and appreciate it. Just as you might find a drawing you made as a youngster and put it on your refrigerator to enjoy in your now adult life, you can find the coping mechanism that your child-self made to keep you safe and enjoy it in your present life. Unlike the drawing that recently resurfaced, you have used this skill throughout your life without knowing it. It has become a natural response. Perhaps you learned to problem-solve quickly or calculate numbers with ease. Whatever the mechanism your child-self honed, you can bring it to your current awareness and value it as a superpower.

Another way to prolong the sensation of feeling most like your SELF is by harnessing your power to wound. The power to wound is a free giveaway your Synthetic Self offers to ensure others treat you as poorly as your Synthetic Self's programming dictates. The power to wound is the key to your emotional closet and, until now, your Synthetic Self has had full access. Your power to wound, in a nutshell, is your permission. When you hand your power to wound to another person, you give them permission to hurt you, and everything becomes personal. It is your personal power you have placed in their hands. Another's Synthetic Self will gladly use your personal power, especially when it's offered freely, to wound you into being 'less than' while they appear to be more.

The dynamic formed when you offer your power to wound, and another takes it to validate their Synthetic Self is a parasite/host relationship. For as long as you, as the host, have something to give, the parasite will use it for its own benefit. By holding on to your power to wound and consciously reclaiming your personal power, the parasitic Synthetic Self of others will walk right by. Your power to wound becomes your power to choose and a power you can trust in.

To trust the Natural Self is to identify your power to wound, the key to your emotional closet, and learn to keep it close. By maintaining your power to wound, it plants your feet so no one can knock you over emotionally. When you stand in the Natural Self, in a way you feel most like yourself, with the key to your emotional closet close, you can finally put your guard down and trust the inner strength of your Natural Self to hold you up.

Another step in learning to trust your Natural Self is to trust your gut. The 'gut reaction' is your body's reaction to a situation. It stems from your instincts, despite a lack of logic or reasoning to back it up. It is the reaction of your body and your senses, of your entire being. It is your truth. The obligation, habit, and firm hand of conditioning come second. The truth of your Natural Self is your immediate response to anything you face. It is direct, precise, and clear. It is instant. But it only lasts for a split second. Once the Synthetic Self gets wind of what is happening, it steps in, enveloping the moment in limitations. Which is why the pause between stimulus and response is so critical. For in that pause lays the power to listen to your gut and make deliberate choices that feel good from there. Decisions that are void of fear, conditioning, and attachment.

Permission is all it takes to trust the Natural Self and open the infinite possibilities for your life. To open the possibilities for your life, you need only be open to the possibilities. You must give yourself permission to step out of the shadows. You must stop waiting for someone to tell you that you deserve it. Stop waiting for the outside world to pave the way. Stop looking for permission outside of SELF and choose to rise from within. You must release all that does not serve the highest SELF and say it out loud! "*I keep all that is true to me and my highest good and release all that is not. I am open to receiving all the possibilities for my life!*" You must stand tall and belt it out so the entire Universe can get on board. When you trust everything that happens is for your highest good, you open yourself to whatever happens next. All that supports, accepts, and serves your highest SELF will enter your life and all that does not will slowly and silently fade away.

This is the tricky part, allowing all that does not serve your highest good to leave your life. People will leave, jobs will end, doors will close and there will be a period of silence. In that silence, you must keep the trust going and give the Universe time to return your life to its natural path. It will seem endless, especially if you are used to a go-go-go and do-do-do lifestyle. But the Natural Self is about being, not doing. Trust that things are moving behind the scenes. The story of your life rests in the hands of your decision to trust fully and completely in the highest version of SELF. You must keep the trust. For the minute you abandon it is the minute the Synthetic Self reclaims its hold with all its limitations and beliefs.

In your Natural Self, you trust that the purpose of life is to live for your greatest and highest good. This means that adversity, resistance and the word 'no' are a wake-up call. Only the Synthetic Self sees rejection. The Natural Self sees 'no' as a detour sign designed to let you know the path is not for your highest good. The word 'no' simply states 'do not go this way. There is a better path for you.' The Natural Self trusts that everything happens for a reason and that reason is to teach you to live in your highest SELF. All that feels light and exciting, embrace. Anything that feels heavy and causes a heavy sigh to escape your lips and your shoulders to slump, walk away from. Paying attention to the body becomes an empowering lifestyle choice. Trusting your truth does not come overnight. It is a series of conscious choices made every moment of every day. If you make conscious choices that feel good, your truth and life will naturally follow.

You must stand at arm's length in any situation, intercept your typical patterns and reactions, and observe. If you only changed one thing, let it be observing rather than searching your ingrained database. Imagine going for a job interview and stepping into the interviewer's office. There are papers piled high on the desk. The minute they see you, they begin digging through the papers. They are so consumed with this search they do not acknowledge you or ask questions. After 5 minutes of head down searching, the interviewer, without looking at you, suggests that if you hadn't come early, they would have had your resume in hand. If you didn't interrupt them by saying hello, they would have found it already. After 10 minutes, the interviewer shows visible signs of agitation and barks at you to stop watching them. After 15 minutes, the interviewer finally stops searching long enough to tell you that you are not a good fit for the company. Then they tell you to leave. The interviewer has attacked your character to redirect their Synthetic Self from the shame of disorganization, absent-mindedness, and chaos it has created for itself. Leaving your Synthetic Self completely baffled. For, in its programming, you show up for an interview and the interviewer asks a series of questions to determine your suitability for the job. But there is no reference point for a scenario like this. So, your Synthetic Self mentally attacks the interviewer for presenting a situation outside your proven programming, grumbling away about the waste of time, the disorganization, and the disrespect the interviewer displayed. Your emotions rise, wreaking havoc on your psyche and body.

Your Natural Self, however, views the scenario quite differently. It sees two individuals crossing paths to exchange information that may assist both in becoming greater beings. Your Natural Self experiences an AH-HA moment, knowing that this was all for your highest good and that the job was not the right path for you to follow. The observer role of your Natural Self immediately identifies the interviewer's Synthetic Self in action and breathes a sigh of relief at not having to work in such a devaluing environment with such a devaluing person. Your Natural Self can then wish the interviewer well, walk away and never look back, grateful for being shown the big picture.

Trust in your Natural Self leaves you open to exploring all possibilities without judgment, expectation or attachment to outcome. When you trust in your SELF, you adopt a new lens. Through this lens, nothing is personal. You view each experience and interaction as a teachable moment designed to lead you through your personal evolution. Through this lens, you accept the learning with the grace of innate wisdom, knowing that all is exactly as it should be. When you trust in your SELF, you trust its path, whatever that looks like, wherever it leads. Through the lens of the Synthetic Self, you attempt to control people, circumstances, and outcomes. The need to control does not exist through the Natural Self's lens because it views and accepts each person as being on the path toward their highest good. Only the Synthetic Self tries to rescue another person to salvage its own ego. The Natural Self does not interfere with another's journey. Though people's paths may cross for a time, the Natural Self knows that your path to personal evolution is a path you must take alone.

So, how do you incorporate an unyielding trust in yourself into your everyday life? How do you pay attention to where your power to wound is, trust your Natural Self, be still and *attend to* what feels good and still get the grocery shopping done, the lawn cut, and the laundry folded? How do you be true to SELF while living amidst the constant rumblings of another's Synthetic Self that threatens to drag you down? How do you maintain a higher state of being when the bills are piling up, the kids keep pleading and the family keeps demanding? How do you go to work every day and maintain a higher state of being? How do you defend against the emotional rollercoaster born of antics, comments and subterfuge of the outside world and still preserve your Natural Self's Zen state? Is it any wonder gurus live on the mountain tops?

Trusting the Natural Self is not just reserved for the

gurus. Remember, those gurus started just like you, seeking a greater meaning in their lives. Each person was born with everything they require to be the guru of their life. Now, with your promise released and your Synthetic Self exposed, your guru SELF, your Natural Self is in full view, and you are learning to trust it. Now you must leap. Regardless of what others say, despite your Lower Self's fears, you must leap. You must give up all that you are, for all that you may become. Whatever it looks like, whatever it brings, whatever you may become. You just have to trust it will lead you where you are supposed to go. It's that simple. When you shout YES to this, you are already there. Everything is conspiring to move and remodel your life to suit the regency of your Higher Self. This commitment is not just about shifting perspective, it is a lifestyle choice. Are you willing to take a crazy leap of faith in yourself? Are you ready to trust everything that happens is for your highest good? Are you ready to marvel at yourself, to stand in awe of your potential and abilities? Are you ready to trust in the highest version of SELF when you can't see it? Trust in it, even when you can't feel it. Trust in the highest version of SELF and allow your life to unfold in amazing ways? Remember, like attracts like. How you relate to SELF is a light you cannot hide. So, you might as well shine! To become the guru of your own life, you must be willing. You must leap. You must trust blindly in the highest version of your highest SELF. When you are ready to commit to this, you will meet your guru SELF. The mountain top, well, that's just a question of real estate.

Exercise

The experience of feeling most like your SELF is unique for everyone. The moment you feel it you have accessed your Natural Self. The only way to have this experience is through an encounter with your sacred place. If you have yet to find your sacred place, try this exercise. Visit different natural locations and pay special attention to the reaction of your senses and body in each. Walk in a forest one day and sit by a stream the next. Lay on the grass one day, then head to the lake the next. Take in the sunrise one day and the sunset the next. The place that resonates with you will be obvious. It will stimulate your senses and all else will fall away without you even noticing. Your sacred space will always be in Nature. Be careful not to judge or discount any natural place, for your Natural Self's sacred place may be different than what you pictured.

While you explore different places, have your journal handy and blissfully scribble down each experience, the smells, the sights, the sounds. Record the places in the body where you feel the stress melting away. When you stumble upon your sacred place, feeling good is inevitable. So is the simplicity of SELF when you're there. The experience will be different for each person. This is an important practice if you are determined to change your life. The more time you spend in your Natural Self, the more it encompasses your life. It is that simple.

Once you find your sacred space, be sure to document the experience in your memory and your journal. Then you can integrate that sacred space sensation into other parts of your life. Incorporate it into your workplace or home by introducing a token of your sacred space into those environments. If a forest is your sacred place, bring a leaf or pinecone into your workplace. Put it where you can see it, touch it, smell it and keep the sacred space feeling alive amidst the chaos. If the ocean is your sacred place, put shells on the dashboard of your car or your kitchen windowsill. Carry a token of your sacred place in your pocket. Each time your body experiences that token, you will feel most like your SELF, infusing it into your everyday living. Instead of you taking on the energy of the 'not so good' places, the 'not so good' places will take on the energy of your sacred space.

Exercise

To fully trust your innate truth, you must remind yourself of what that is and where it comes from. This exercise will do just that. Take yourself to your outdoor sacred space to ensure you are feeling most like yourself and can sit peacefully for a time without interruption. Before you go, locate a photograph of yourself between 3-5 years old that you can take with you.

In your sacred space, take a moment to look around and familiarize yourself with your surroundings. Then close your eyes and recreate your surroundings in your mind. Imagine that a person appears just beyond the border of your sacred space and starts slowly walking toward you. You recognize the person and start slowly walking toward them. As the distance between you closes, you identify the person as a child. It is your child-self from the photograph. The minute you recognize your child-self, you break into a run and scoop the child up into your arms. Still holding the child, you return to your original seat within your sacred space. You both rejoice in being reunited after being separated for many years. It is amazing! As the emotion dissolves, you ask the child about their life. Where they live. What their life is like and listen while they describe the house they live in, and the people raising them. The child talks of their siblings, their pets, their toys, and the trinkets they hold dear. You listen as they speak and find your memories come flooding back.

This child amazes you. They are so full of life and love. The child has a great passion, a fascination they can't stop talking about. It is a talent, hobby or interest and they talk about it with enthusiasm. The child is radiant and alive. You are proud to know them, and even prouder to be them! Immediately, all you learned about yourself in childhood disappears as you embrace this wondrous child and vow to keep them alive in everything you do.

When you return home, keep the photograph of that child with you. Carry it from room to room in your house and chat with the child as if they are right there by your side. Consciously acknowledge, listen to and respect the child in you, healing the hurts and misunderstandings from childhood and building a new relationship with your child-self. Your childlike enthusiasm is re-ignited. This child reflects your Natural Self, and you embrace this part of you.

Over time, you will not require the photograph to conjure up your child-self. You will consider them always. You ask for their advice and consider their feelings and opinions. You can see that this sensitive child did not evolve into an adult, as you would have assumed. Instead, the adult you formed around and over your child-self, like a suit of armor, covering them completely and drowning out their voice. Yet your child-self is just as you left them; a beautiful, naive, loving little kid, shocked by injustice and cruelty, creative, intelligent beyond their years and highly perceptive. This child doesn't miss a thing. They notice the tiniest detail in voice tone, body language and facial expressions and see through to people's souls.

Trusting your Natural Self begins with re-visiting the child you were and getting re-acquainted. Now, in wisdom, you can discard what you blindly accepted as a child. Now in wisdom, you can choose what to believe, what makes sense to you, for you and you can openly choose to discard all that does not serve your highest SELF.

10

12 SIMPLE WAYS TO STAY TRUE TO YOURSELF EVERY DAY

"Life is a day-by-day experiment in being authentic."
-Sky Stevens

To reclaim the power of SELF and fully trust all that you innately are, you must give up all hope of a better past. You cannot change it. Nor can you change how others choose to show up in this world. Once you fully understand these two concepts, you can then turn your energy toward being the best version of SELF you can be. With these twelve simple ways to keep you trusting SELF, you can discover your ingenuity and strength and take ownership of all the wonderful pieces of yourself that have been hidden for so long.

These twelve simple ways to keep you trusting SELF reveal how easy it is to live comfortably in the Natural Self. Like anything new, these practices may feel awkward at first because they challenge your Synthetic Self's limitations, your comfort zone. Yet, with repetition, these will empower you, if you let go of the past, to reclaim your present life. For you to feel empowered, you must have complete faith in the highest version of SELF and trust it to steer your life. You must identify, take ownership of, and give attention and power to SELF. The following assist you in doing just that. They reveal the version of yourself that you have always known was there and provide a fun and easy way to build the courage to step into it, ridding yourself of the emotional roller coaster of the Synthetic Self by contesting the Covert belief in real-time. For the following to be effective, you must view each as an adventure, have fun with them and revel in finding the strength and joy in all that is your Natural Self.

1. Set The Stage

The set design of your life can make or break your production and reveal many things about you, the main character, on your life's stage. It offers a physical environment that supports your story as it unfolds and reveals the truth within. The set design of your daily life includes your personal space, clothing, posture, and habitat. These are the elements of your current way of being. Just as a captivating stage design enhances the story the actors portray, so do the elements of your daily life enhance either the Synthetic Self or the Natural Self, depending on which is steering your life. For change to happen, you must change the set design to enhance the new story.

Start with your posture. It is something most don't think about, but it tells your inner story from a distance. Everyone has witnessed a person walking with their eyes to the ground, shoulders rounded, head down, hands in their pockets. Someone who wears dark colors and barely acknowledges others as they pass. And everyone has witnessed the person who walks with a spring in their step and their head held high, greeting everyone with eye contact and a big smile. Your posture translates what you believe about your SELF into a language the outside world can understand. Your posture is a billboard. Not only does it advertise, but it leaves a lasting impression. Does your body stand tall, ready to take on life with style and grace? Or is it hunched over, making itself as small as possible, hoping to stay under the radar? Does your posture reflect a person who trusts in and honors their highest SELF? If not, you can adopt a new posture that does. You can pay attention when you walk to where your eyes fall. Are they surveying the ground? It is time to keep your eyes on the horizon and your body open to receive all a good life offers.

From the back of the theater, imagine the story your clothing tells as you walk on stage. Do your clothes reflect a person alive, awesome, happy, and confident? Go to your closet and pick out the piece of clothing that is your favorite, the one that makes you feel most like yourself. Clothing is a great identifier of all that lies beneath. With that one favorite piece hanging on a door or in a place of prominence, you can review the rest of your wardrobe. Do you wear everything in your closet? Have you handpicked each item to reflect the highest version of SELF? Or have you allowed your Synthetic Self to assign a wardrobe that validates its presence?

Your Synthetic Self repeats its wardrobe as it repeats its old patterns. There may be a variety of colors, yet the items of clothing are the same. Perhaps the style of clothing varies, but the color is the same. Possibly there is a variety of clothing and colors, but they represent a long-ago era and are now stretched out of shape with the color faded. Your Synthetic Self will often purchase the same item in five different colors or the same color in five different items. If this is present in your current wardrobe, it is time to revamp. You must wear what highlights the highest version of SELF. When you wear what feels good, what makes you feel most like yourself, you represent your SELF authentically. You must lose every piece of clothing that covers up your radiance or redirects others away from it.

Are there items cast to the back of your closet in desperate need of repair, with zippers broken or holes needing mending? Or are there forgotten items that have slipped off hangers and fallen to the floor unnoticed? These all reflect your self-image. If you are to stop hiding your Natural Self, the hidden identity at the back of the closet must stop hiding as well.

If there are clothes in your closet with slogans and sayings, these require examination. From the back of the theater, do those slogans enhance your authentic SELF or hide you behind a billboard for John Deere or Nike? Do they sport words or phrases that support your dreams and goals for life or business? Even if a t-shirt was free, when its slogan takes away from or diminishes you when you wear it, it must go. Phrases and sayings that genuinely resonate with or advertise your Natural Self and remind you to remain authentic can stay.

The same goes for trends. Trends feed conformity. Worn like armor, trends ensure individuals blend in with the masses, invisible, and unseen. A baseball cap and sunglasses cover most of the face, allowing you a tainted view out and closing off any who would look in. Bright, flashy accessories pull the attention away from your authentic SELF when you wear them. To live an empowered life, you must own your natural radiance and wear it proudly. You should be conscious of using trends and accessories to satiate the Synthetic Self's need for validation. These only keep your dynamic Natural Self hidden from sight.

Although humans are not thought of as building habitats, they certainly do. Your habitat includes the choice of shelter, decor, furnishings, color, cleanliness, and upkeep. Whether your habitat is one room or a mansion, the conditioning of the Synthetic Self is easy to detect there. Some crowd their space with the fruits of their labor; artwork they've created, photographs they've taken, furniture they've made. While others sport the local Ikea showroom. Some create a space that they feel good in, while others create a space to impress others. Some strive to satiate the Synthetic Self with the TV remote affixed to one recliner, an empty fridge and a counter topped with takeout boxes, while others build a space for the gathering of many. Some blanket their space with the past (grandma's egg cup collection, Great-Aunt Bessie's crocheting on every surface, photographs of deceased family and friends) with a minimal representation of those who presently dwell there. Some paint their space in the same prominent color as the clothing they wear. Some keep a clean and organized space, while others pile their space high with boxes and totes lining the hallways. As the Synthetic Self becomes habitual over time, so does the practice of habitat. The clutter of the mind creates a cluttered space. The indifference in SELF magnifies indifference in your space. The celebrating of you creates a celebrated space. How you embed the Synthetic Self into your habitat speaks volumes.

From the back of the theater, your habitat is the set design that gives depth and meaning to your story. You must look at your habitat objectively and be honest about it. If you do not feel the most like yourself in it, then you need to change it. It is time to get rid of anything and everything that does not symbolize, enhance or promote your highest SELF. The more truth you can bring to your space, the more authentic it will be. The closer you are to your Natural Self and purpose. The more like-minded folks you will meet. The happier and more fulfilled your life will be. You must ensure your personal space and everything in it reflects the perfect set design for the highest version of SELF and watch your Natural Self shine.

The personal space you have around your body reflects the level of trust you have in your authentic being. To really dive into the process of owning your personal space, you can take a journal to a local coffee shop, grocery store or bench on a downtown street and observe people. Young, old, male, female, you can observe them all. Do not judge. Notice the vibe people convey and what emotion rouses in you while observing each person. What is it about their movements, interactions or how they carry themselves that stirs an internal reaction in you? Do not meet these people or interact with them. Just observe.

You can then turn to a blank page in your journal and draw a line across the page vertically and horizontally, making four equal sections. In the upper left section of the page, you can write what you experience while observing others. Does a person welcome others in or push them away? Do they seem cold and aloof, or warm and inviting? Is their personal space accepting and supportive, or unpleasant and dishonoring? Is it kind and comforting, or abrupt and trivializing? To be effective, you must pay particular attention to the qualities in others you enjoy, admire, or feel drawn to. You can also note your body language during this process. What is it about another's personal space that makes you sit back to distance yourself or lean forward to close the space? What makes you want to walk away from or toward another person? Notice yourself and the type of personal space you appreciate and respond to in a positive way.

Now objectively view your personal space. In the upper right section, write a quick descriptor of how you see your personal space. Does it welcome others in or push others away? Is it cold and aloof, or warm and inviting? Is it accepting and supportive, or unpleasant and dishonoring? Is it kind and comforting, or abrupt and trivializing? It is time to be honest. You won't be doing yourself any favors by pretending to be something that you are not. Own your personal space just as it is. Embrace the good, the bad and the ugly. Describe it as accurately as possible. Consider yourself a person like the ones you previously observed. What would your personal space reveal? If you could define your personal space in one word, what would it be?

If you want to take this further, here is an experiment. Return to the local coffee shop, grocery store or bench on a downtown street and interact with others. Say hello to people around you or approach the counter and order something and notice how others react to you. Do they lean in or back away? Pay attention to the silent impact your personal space has on others. If you stand close to another person, does the other person remain or step back? Does the other person offer a dirty look or smile? It is important to fully appreciate the impression your personal space offers and what it communicates. Write it all down and take full ownership of it.

After filling the upper quadrants of the page, move to the bottom two sections. In the bottom left quadrant, write out a description of your ideal personal space (You can refer to the list of qualities you admire in others if needed). What would you like it to look like and feel like to others? Describe what you would like others to experience as they approach and interact with you, and the image left after you walk away. If there was one word scrolled across the welcome mat at the entrance of your personal space, what would it be?

Re-read your original description of your personal space in the top right and compare it to your ideal in the bottom left. In the bottom right quadrant, write a list of what you can change about or within your personal space to show up in a more authentic way.

2. Get Outside

The relationship you have with Nature reflects the relationship you have with SELF. How you relate to the Natural Self, the person you innately are, is how you relate to Nature. If you deny your Natural Self, you deny Nature's abundance in your life. If you fear your true power and elegance, you will fear Nature as well. Spending time around life forms that are fulfilling their purpose allows you to resonate with your true purpose. Remember, like attracts like. What better way to trust your innate beauty than to surround yourself with beauty that is innate? Lay on the grass and let the Earth heal your body. Listen to the birds or insects. Watch the clouds roll by like you did as a kid. Hug a tree. Take in a sunset. Marvel at the smell of a flower. Nature is a cornucopia of healing, from herbs and plants, from fruit to grains, from animal medicines to energy. It is the only beautiful thing that truly nourishes your body and your mind.

When you stand at the back of the theater and view a set design filled with poison for mice, swatters for flies, traps for bees, zappers for insects and an array of chemical compounds to annihilate every plant from sidewalks and driveways, would you stay to watch the production? Killing, trapping, destroying and poisoning may allow for a complex illusion of power, however, it does not broadcast an abundant life.

The energy you need is in Nature. The Earth offers energy freely and will heal your body and your mind. It will connect you to your innate being through your sacred place. Man-made spaces are not conducive to decompressing. They are energetic cesspools, keeping the Synthetic Self stimulated. Nature is there, ready and waiting. Though many people express an appreciation for Nature, very few interact with it directly. Walking from the house to the car is not the same as sitting by a stream. Watching birds from the living room window is not the same as sitting in a forest. A landscaped screen saver is not the same as standing on a mountain. The Natural Self is innate, organic, and genuine. It is not man-made, so man-made environments or devices cannot nurture it. The Natural Self doesn't care what the neighbors think, it trusts its nature. It doesn't care if the Earth gets its clothes dirty. It has no fear of bugs or birds. Connecting with Nature is truly the most natural thing a person can do. After all, humans are a species of Nature.

Being out in Nature for even 30 minutes every day is beneficial to your mind and spirit. You will be more present, more fulfilled, more conscious, more satisfied, more of who you innately are. Interacting with the great outdoors brings your whole being into focus. For some, it may be a forest where the smells and sounds instantly allow the shoulders to drop and the tension to dissolve. For others, it may be the ocean where you can dip toes in and feel the rush of tranquility throughout your entire body. Others may find a mountain trail sacred. Where each step serves to clear your mind and ground you. Wherever your sacred place is, you must go often.

As you trust your Natural Self, you will also trust Nature. Nature does not ask for attention. Its power, beauty, and purpose are authentic and raw. As you introduce yourself to Nature, you open SELF up to who you naturally are. As you get to know your beauty and strength, you see the beauty and strength in Nature. These go hand in hand. Go outside and frequent the place where you feel most like yourself. Sit at the base of a tree and breathe for a moment. Walk by a river and allow the sounds to drown out the echoes of abuse, anger, and resentment. Go to the ocean and dance, unleashing the emotion that has prevented you from moving forward. Do not underestimate the impact Nature can have on your psyche or the comfort it can offer. When you see and feel the rhythm of Nature, you will see and feel the rhythm of your abundant life.

3. Be Deliberate With Language

The Natural Self selects words that honestly reveal SELF in the moment. The Synthetic Self uses language to create an illusion. When it needs validation, the Synthetic Self boasts and brags. When it needs sympathy, it lists ailments and injustices. Trusting a life in your Natural Self is trusting SELF enough to accurately select your words. To say what you mean and mean what you say. It takes courage and practice. You may feel vulnerable while you get the hang of it. That is okay. Start by eliminating the words *should, always* and *never.* These words keep you stuck in the old patterns, habits, and programming of the Synthetic Self. The word *can't,* casts you in the ensemble, not as the star of your life story, so eliminate that too. The more you trust in SELF, the more authentic your language becomes, the more you live in your Natural Self.

Do not make promises, ever. A promise is an excuse for the Synthetic Self to betray who you innately are and continue all the second-guessing that comes from the fear of stepping into and owning your true glory and power.

4. Notice What Is Noticed

There are signposts along every road. The path to your Natural Self is no exception. These signposts are subtle, hand-selected, and visible only to you. They reveal your next steps. They are always there, yet only visible when you pay attention. By capturing your attention, they bring inspiration and teach you to trust your instincts. Wherever you go, whatever you do, note what pulls your attention. What you observe without meaning to. Maybe you're sitting in a meeting and instead of listening, you gaze at a poster on the wall. Suddenly, you are inspired to embark on a creative project. Perhaps you are driving and notice a cat on the sidewalk. Suddenly, you get the answer to the question you asked the day before. By noticing what you notice, how and why it has captured your attention, and the result, you will see beyond the immediate and accept inspiration as it comes. How you notice and what you notice will be unlike anyone else, so you can trust it is for your highest good. There can be an inspiration in anything. There can be answers in the mundane. And solutions in the concealed. Pay attention to what captures your attention and trust what shows up. There could be a message in a painting, clarity in a magazine, brilliance in a billboard. Anything can trigger the Natural Self to shine through. By noticing what you notice, you experience your Natural Self's inspiration and direction. You can trust that.

There are always things to notice. Even as you read this book, you experience many things. The most obvious is, of course, reading, yet you might also experience the familiar warmth of a pet beside you, the texture of the couch you're sitting on, the coolness of the evening air, or the warmth of the sun. Perhaps you experience the crunch of a snack you're enjoying as you read, the fruity tang of a glass of wine, or the faint gurgle of the fish tank in the next room. Each of these sensations offers an experience to be embraced.

Close your eyes and note all you are experiencing at this moment. Listen. Smell. Taste. Touch. There is so much more to your life than the limited encounters of the Synthetic Self. Are you physically comfortable? Are you sitting, lying down, or standing? Are you smelling the lingering aroma of freshly baked bread or taking in the smells of a garden as you read? Perhaps you are traveling on a bus or airplane? Are you warm or cold? The more you engage the senses, the more present you become and the more conscious of every level of your being.

5. Listen To The Body

Your body will communicate everything you need to know to trust your Natural Self. All you have to do is listen. The physical body doubles as your emotional closet. It stores the emotions from childhood which, over time, cause an imbalance, a dis-ease in your physical form. The bladder, gallbladder, spleen and skin, the liver, kidneys, stomach and heart, are all storage containers used by the Synthetic Self. With the digestive tract carrying the load of all that is unresolved. To unburden yourself from the past and trust your innate power, you must locate the exact place in your body where your Synthetic Self has stored the emotion it was unable or unwilling to deal with. Your body will announce the dis-ease in a specific location. For example, if your childhood promise reflects giving your power away, the body will push the weight of responsibility away, leaving the physical form underweight and easily broken, like the self-image. If your promise reflects taking responsibility for others, the body absorbs the weight of everyone's burden, leaving it obese, labored and unmovable. When you trust in SELF and live in the balance of the Natural Self, your body reflects a natural state of balance and weight. By uncovering and owning the emotions from long ago, you can unleash the past from the container, freeing your organs up to work efficiently and restoring ease in your body.

The body is also your truth barometer. It will keep you grounded in your truth. All you have to do is ask and apply the Light/Heavy Principle. Despite the Synthetic Self overshadowing this innate feature of the body, your body has always had this ability to speak to you. With every stimulus that comes, your body will generate a light or heavy response. It will either react to situations and language with a light sensation (happy, excited, thrilled or energized) or a heavy one (burdened, troubled, or hampered). If you decide on a course of action and feel light as a result, you know you are standing in the truth of your Natural Self. However, if your body feels heavy, your shoulders slump, a hefty sigh escapes your lips, and you immediately start looking for a way out, your body is telling you this decision is not in your highest good.

Take, for example, if you receive an invitation to an anniversary celebration of a friend. Before answering, you can check in with the body using the Light/Heavy Principle. Do you feel honored by the invite, excited about the event, and offer help or support to your friend? Or do you sigh, feel your shoulders slump, and immediately start conjuring up some excuse not to go? Or worse, recognize the heavy sensation generated by the invitation, but allow the Synthetic Self to convince you to go to the party out of an obligation to reciprocate since your friend attended a past event of yours when asked. Second-guessing, justifying, and excusing reflect the programming of the Synthetic Self.

The Light/Heavy Principle can also distinguish which people within your daily life support your Natural Self, and which do not. In the presence of each person, do you feel light, joyous, and happy? Or do you secretly dread that person's company? Feel heavy, burdened and drained around the person and exhausted by them? The Light/Heavy Principle is the voice of the Natural Self. You must trust it. Your body knows if the personal relationships in your current life align with your highest good or keep you stuck in the Synthetic Self. If you feel drained and exhausted around someone, it is time to say goodbye, opening a space for new and uplifting folks to enter your life.

You can also apply the Light/Heavy Principle to the past. Whether something happened yesterday, last week, or long ago, a trip down memory lane can stir emotion and leave calamity in its wake. If the sediment filters through the Natural Self's lens, it results in a contemplative smile with a light and happy mood, and all is good. If the emotional residue leaves you feeling small, victimized, resentful, or angry, the Synthetic Self's lens is at work. The Natural Self views events of the past as stepping stones that brought you to this moment. It understands the past is not personal and never was. It only becomes personal through the Synthetic Self's lens because the Synthetic Self must keep its anchor attached to the child-self that created it. Therefore, it keeps its programming alive by replaying all the things you could have said or should have done. Spiraling your mind down into the ooze of victimhood with its ceaseless chatter and keeping your child-self at the mercy of another's actions. It leaves your child-self waiting for the past to change, for others to see the error of their ways, for others to think differently, act differently, and be different. The Synthetic Self will pick any memory of any era to manipulate through this lens. Meanwhile, you are losing sleep over it, not eating over it, or eating too much over it. To the Synthetic Self, the past is just as accessible as the present for keeping you stuck in its programming, and it will use whatever it can.

Lightness comes when you trust your Natural Self and accept that the past will not change no matter how long you replay it, how many cookies you eat, how many days you stay in bed, or how destructive you are to yourself or others. Holding on to something that will not change is like a drowning man grabbing the water to save him. The past is a means to an end. A path that led you to this moment, and in this moment, you can choose how to spend your time, energy, and strength.

The Light/ Heavy Principle will distinguish the Natural Self from the Synthetic Self. Through it, the body will show whether you are being sucked back into the Synthetic Self or trusting the Natural Self. The Synthetic Self will convince you to make yourself small with its programming that says, "But they did that to me". It fills you with the heavy burden of being at another's mercy. While the Natural Self says, "They might very well have, but now I have a choice. Do I choose to play the leading role in my story or the victim in someone else's?".

6. Own What Goes In

What you see, touch, taste, smell, hear and are moved by impacts how you feel, how you think, and how you interact with your life. This motivates your choices. Anything you watch, read and/or witness that engages your senses, impacts how you think and feel, and determines if you surrender to the Synthetic Self or permit yourself to live in the Natural Self.

Whether it be movies, books, television or social media, you must choose wisely, for what goes in has an incredible impact on your perception of SELF. For example, if you decide to build a new front porch, suddenly you notice the front porch of every house you see. When you desire a new hairstyle, suddenly you notice every person's hair. When you watch a horror film, suddenly you hear bumps in the night that get the adrenaline pumping. When you read a novel about blame and revenge in a predator/prey dynamic, suddenly you get defensive, and suspicious, feel attacked, and accuse others or pick a fight. Or when you watch the TV news relentlessly, suddenly you adopt the opinions, concerns, convictions and certainties depicted there at an almost aggressive speed and challenge those around you to know what you know and believe what you believe, even though none of it comes from your experience directly. In short, your focus becomes your reality.

It doesn't matter where you come from, what nationality you are, or how much money you have, the more attention you give to something, the more influence it has over your life. Some would argue that books, television, movies and social media are merely entertainment, yet what you give your attention to shows what is important to spend your time and energy on. The Universe sees this and says, *"Oh, that's what is important to them? Ok, let's give them more of that."* So, choose your influences carefully and consciously.

You must watch, read and/or witness themes that depict the direction you want to go, that influence, motivate, empower and excite you toward living in the highest version of SELF. If living an authentic life in your Natural Self is your desire, choose to watch, read and/or witness themes that depict a person discovering who they truly are. If you desire a better relationship with your grown-up kids, watch, read and/or witness themes that depict the reuniting of family. If you wish to increase your income or wealth, watch, read and/or witness themes that depict rags to riches. You must observe the influences that currently hold your attention and energy and decide if these accurately depict where you want to go or the life you wish for yourself. If what you currently watch, read and/or witness does not promote your highest good, it is time to shift your attention and energy to something that does.

7. Find The Joy

The absolute best method for trusting your Natural Self is to find joy in all you do. Even if you feel compelled to do something you don't want to do, you can find the joy. Sometimes, joy is not obvious because your Synthetic Self focuses on the negative, the drudgery of the task at hand to keep you limited. But by repeating *'Find the joy'*, your perspective will soon shift. Remember, your focus becomes your reality. So, if you focus on experiencing joy in every moment and every task, the joy will find you.

One way to find the joy is to make 'responding' an art form. Instead of reacting, stand tall, shoulders back, take a deep slow breath and be still. Then, respond from a bigger place, in a thoughtful way, with all the grace of the highest version of SELF and find the joy of your Natural Self's radiance and magnificence.

8. Eat From The Earth

It is very simple. Synthetic food feeds the Synthetic Self. Natural food nourishes the Natural Self. The body is a machine. It needs the proper fuel to run efficiently. Food provided by the Earth is full of vitamins and nutrients, amino acids, minerals, and so much more. Highly processed, synthetic, man-made foods, not so much. Sure, there may be an infusion of minerals or an injection of vitamins, but if the Earth did not grow the product in soil, where did it come from? Can you expect the body to run efficiently on prepared chemicals that, instead of growing up a vine, come down a conveyor belt? When you step off the Synthetic Self's conveyor belt and trust your Natural Self, the body, the emotions and weight return to their natural state. The Synthetic Self lives in the aisles of the grocery store with synthetic man-made food. While the Natural Self lives around the perimeter with the foods grown in and on the Earth.

9. Ruin Routine

A routine is a sequence of actions followed repeatedly. In short, a fixed program. Some routines are necessary. For example, when following doctor's orders or those occurring in certain occupations. However, routines set out by the programming of the Synthetic Self can keep you on *auto-pilot*. The Synthetic Self thrives on its fixed program and thus employs routine to keep it in place. To trust your Natural Self, you must interrupt, break, and destroy the programming of the Synthetic Self.

Destroying the Synthetic Self's programming begins with ruining the routines you are no longer conscious of. Typically, those at the beginning and end of the day are the most ingrained and a great place to begin. Observe each step of your evening routine and then deliberately mix it up. Brush your teeth with your non-dominant hand. Comb your hair with your back to the mirror. Floss your teeth without looking at all. Put bedtime clothing on in the opposite order with the opposite arm in first. Or better still, sleep in something entirely different or nothing at all. Read out loud instead of in silence. All this may seem silly and awkward, but then again, that is the point. To rock your world and un-lodge you from the mindless repeating of the Synthetic Self's mechanical action.

You mustn't stop there. You must ruin your morning routine as well. Put your favorite mug at the back of the cupboard and use a different one. Tie your shoes with your eyes closed. If you normally have silence in the mornings, put music on and boogie while getting dressed. If you typically turn the TV on first thing, try moving about in silence. Go out the back door instead of the front. Take a different route to work each day and park in a different spot. Smile. Laugh. Explore your humanness and celebrate it. When you challenge yourself to do things differently, the results will amaze and excite you, inviting you to try even more new things.

Every day for one week, do each routine task differently. Try cooking instead of takeout. Reading instead of television. Try sleeping in front of the fireplace even if you need to work the next day. Try dancing in the kitchen or having a picnic on the living room floor. As you go through your day, pay attention. When you perform a routine task like brushing your teeth, making coffee or feeding the dog, change it up. Try saying no when you'd typically say YES.

Open your closet and close your eyes. See if you can distinguish each item simply by touch. Eat ice cream with a fork or salad with your hands. Close the fridge with your hip. Swing on a swing. Hug a tree. Sing with the radio and belt it out. Play air guitar. Appreciate the silliness of dancing in your underwear. Revel in the experience of eating your dinner with soft music and candlelight. In short, for the next week, ROCK YOUR WORLD! Allow yourself to lighten up. Laugh. Dance. Be kind to yourself and find the joy. Invite others to join in if you'd like. If you are smiling as you read this, you are halfway there!

Rocking your world is simply about exercising your power to turn everyday experiences into sensational ones. The Natural Self is a master at this. The Natural Self is constantly looking for ways to be amazed by what it is capable of. To live a richer and fuller life, you must live life in a richer and fuller way. For one day, turn off the phone, unplug the television, close the laptop and allow yourself the luxury of simply spending the day with SELF. Eat when you're hungry, sleep when you're tired, and allow your world to flow naturally. One day, out of the stream, out of the chaos, to lose touch. No timeline. No interruption. Explore to the edge of your character and marvel at yourself. And above all, revel in all that you are and all you are capable of. It will amaze you!

10. Hand Pick Companions

What society considers a common exchange of introduction and niceties is really a quick tutorial on how you feel about yourself. You can tell how someone feels about themselves by how you feel when you are with them. So, take note. How you feel around another person is your Natural Self, revealing the truth to you and their Synthetic Self revealing its programming. When you meet someone friendly, gentle and respectful, you can be sure they respect and cherish themselves. When you meet someone distant and standoffish, the person is communicating how little they invest in themselves and how little they will invest in you. When someone appears negative, or victimized, recounts ailments, complaints, and wrongdoings against them, they harbor a promise to be a victim. Everything and everyone have power over them, and they are inviting you to buy into their drama. By sympathizing, you take the bait. Their ailments and the wrongdoings against them have become their sales pitch, their marketing, the worm on their hook baiting each person to bite. Consider each person carefully and learn to observe the Synthetic Self behind the scenes. Do not waste time with people you would not change places with.

11. Take Center Stage

Do not play second to anyone, including your Synthetic Self. Your life is your story. Who else should play the leading role but you? You can consciously choose to isolate yourself from the shame of being different. Or you can embrace what is unique, valuable and different about you and stand in that power.

Treat yourself like someone worth dating, worth getting to know and worth falling in love with. It doesn't matter what stage of life you are in; living a life that feels good can begin anytime. So, dress yourself up and take yourself out! If you live with others, boldly announce you have a date with your highest SELF and go. Nurture a relationship with yourself. Sit with SELF on the couch and watch a movie. Snuggle up and read a book out loud. Blast the music and dance with SELF in the kitchen. Mail

SELF letters and greeting cards. Buy SELF flowers. You cannot play the leading role in your own story until you give yourself the leading role. Take the time to have a relationship with SELF; light candles for your SELF and cook SELF a glorious meal. Take in a sunset or a walk in the park. Learn from SELF, teach SELF new things, and explore, truly, as if you were someone you were dating. Laugh with SELF. Find humor in your antics. Excite in your tomfoolery. Spend time with SELF, get to know SELF and you will learn what your truth is and how to speak it. Have fun with it. Enjoy the experience. If someone asks what your plans are for tonight, tell them your plans include a candlelight dinner for you. Sure, some may laugh, but they are laughing because they would never think to honor or embrace themselves in such a way.

12. Write It All Down

One of the best ways to observe your thinking is to journal. Journaling gets rid of the chatter in the mind and opens your perspective. Computers and smartphones will not cut it this time. Find a journal you like and decorate the cover with your intention for the year. Get a special pen or colored markers and make journaling an event. Paste things in, draw, color, sketch, or practice calligraphy. Have fun with it. What better way to celebrate you than to create an occasion to honor your thoughts, perspective, use of words and creativity? Start with one word. Whatever word pops into your mind. Write that one word down and then just keep writing. Journaling offers great clarity. It offers ownership and understanding of the way you think and feel. It's like spring cleaning for the closet of the mind.

The closet of your mind is the one place no one else has access to. No husband, wife, sibling, or parent; no one else has access to your inner world. You cannot make another react, speak or behave, despite the society-approved language that suggests otherwise. Blaming an event, situation or person for your Synthetic Self is, well, like blaming the ocean for making your feet wet. Each person can choose what they step into or out of. Journaling is a great way to celebrate your mind, explore your choices and find humor in being human.

These twelve simple ways to stay true to yourself help you reclaim the power of SELF every day. They break the invisible chain that binds you to your Synthetic Self. They help you be conscious in every moment and redirect your energy toward being the best version of SELF. By doing these every day, you capture your ingenuity and strength and take ownership of all the wonderful pieces of you.

These twelve simple ways to stay true to yourself give you permission to live comfortably in your Natural Self. With repetition, they will empower you to let go of the old story and reclaim your present. They will teach you to have complete faith in the highest version of SELF (the SELF you have always known was there), giving you the courage to step into a new way of being and trust it to steer your life. Have fun with these twelve simple ways to stay true to yourself and revel in finding the strength and joy in all that is your Natural Self.

Trusting your Natural Self means trusting the innate knowing of SELF based on its truth. Recognizing it as an element of nature, with inherent features, and qualities like instinct, wisdom and intuition. Trusting the Natural Self means trusting your capacity to explore the plane between the visible (the physical form) and the invisible (knowing, reasoning, intellect). Trusting your Natural Self means trusting your perfection. You hold more potential than you realize. Trusting your Natural Self means moving along your path with grace, humility, honor, and integrity. It means being passionate about your existence and finding pure joy in simply being.

ABOUT THE AUTHOR

Raised by a pursuit of image and status, Sky Stevens blindly worked her way up to a corner office with a view, only to find she spent more time gazing out the window, pondering the human dynamic and wondering what else was out there.

With a great leap of faith, she abandoned the only life she had ever known and set out on a quest of Self Un-Covery. She sold her house in the suburbs, her rental property and traded in her four-door hatch-back for an RV and set out on a life-altering, deeply personal, multi-country quest to live an authentic life. Camera, journal and laptop strapped to her side, she started a road-trip blog entitled 'Unwitnessed Life' documenting her personal exploration, revealing the layers of her learned self as she wrote. She soon discovered that the true measure of her success did not lay in the corporate ambitions of her early environment, but in un-covering the messy, authentic beauty of who she was underneath.

As a speaker, facilitator and author of a curriculum-based children's book series Looking Close; Teaching

Kids To Love The Earth, requests poured in for her to facilitate Self Un-Covery workshops. It was here Sky found her true nature, the place she felt most like herself. Her natural humor and authentic voice embracing and deepening the personal journey of her audiences.

In *You Can't Blame Karma*, Sky translates her own journey of Self Un-Covery on to the page, offering readers her firsthand experience of shaving off the layers of a learned self-image to reveal the amazing, authentic person underneath and supporting her readers to release what is holding them back to create the life they truly want.

Printed in the United States
by Baker & Taylor Publisher Services